Interrupted...by God Book Two

by

Doug Pacheco

Full Stature Publishing Interrupted...by God Book Two by Doug Pacheco

Published by IngramSpark ISBN: 979-8-9996610-1-2

Edited by Doug Pacheco

Cover Design by Donna Cook

Contents

Introduction

When I look at world history—and even more so, Bible history—I notice something remarkable: the people God chose to use were often hidden, unknown, cowardly, or just plain loudmouths. My kind of people!

God worked through doubters, shepherds, and even unlikely rich men like Joseph of Arimathea. If Joseph hadn't given away his tomb, we'd never have heard of him. And shepherds announcing the arrival of the Savior?

No one in 21st-century America would have picked them, that's for sure.

David was tucked away in a smelly sheepfold, so unimportant his own father didn't even consider him when Samuel came knocking, looking for a king. Gideon? God found him hiding in a winepress, threshing wheat where wheat was never meant to be threshed.

Who does that? Chicken livers—that's who.

Jonah? He was the guy who basically flipped God off and ran the other way—until God found a fish with more obedience than Jonah and had it swallow him up to deliver him back on track.

What kind of God picks such "losers" to change the world?

Jehovah God—that's who.

He is the God who sees not just what you are, but what you can become. The God who takes glory for Himself—not because He's egotistical, but because

He's the only one worthy of it, the only one who can handle it.

So yes, go ahead and judge your own uselessness. Disqualify yourself because of your inadequacies if you want. But know this: God loves raising up the lowly. He picks the one chosen last for basketball, the dying thief, the soldier with a sick servant, the proud fisherman. He plucks us out of obscurity and gives us His name—and together with Him, we turn the world upside down.

I believe one of the reasons our faith often feels mundane is that instead of being led by the Spirit, we get swept into our busy, hectic lives. We stop paying attention to the adventures God wants to take us on. But interruption was the order of the day in the New Testament.

And God is big on obedience. We can have all sorts of important tasks lined up, but when the Lord interrupts our day, He expects obedience. And when we obey, great things happen. Faithful in little, faithful in much.

Every single time Jesus called His disciples, they were in the middle of their daily routines. Peter, James, and John were fishing. Matthew was collecting taxes. But two others—the rich young ruler and Nicodemus—refused the interruption.

In this second volume, my hope is that you've already decided to obey when the Holy Spirit interrupts. I'll share stories from my own life and from others that show how God's direction often doesn't feel like a conscious "choice" at all—it simply happens as we surrender.

It's so easy to get wrapped up in life that we forget the Giver of life. We get busy and distracted, missing the moments when God is trying to redirect our attention. But we must be willing to let Him interrupt our schedules, even when it stings.

Yes, it's frustrating when plans fall apart (I'll admit I struggle with that myself). But maybe, just maybe, things are going according to plan—just not our plan.

Here's what I've discovered: most of God's interruptions don't come with lightning bolts from the sky. They usually arrive in the middle of ordinary, everyday life—while I'm doing one of the "10,000" mundane tasks that fill a day.

In fact, I can give you a list of when God does His best work:

When you're busy.

When it's inconvenient.

When it requires sacrifice.

When only you and He will know.

When He knows you'll give Him the glory.

When it's the very thing you'd rather not do.

When the interruption reveals a new facet of His character.

Finally, as Christina Fox reminds us:

"It's hard to see all the little frustrating events and interruptions in our day as divinely placed opportunities to grow in grace, but they are. And seeing them as such helps us take our eyes off ourselves and put them on Christ, who cares more about our transformation than about our daily comfort. Rather than giving us a life of ease, he interrupts our lives with grace and shows us what we need most of all: himself."

DEDICATION

To my wife Mary Ann, who married me, loved me and encouraged me to write this book.

They're All Around Us!

People seem to have more crises during holidays that just about any other time.

Something my wife said the other evening struck home with me about the best part of Thanksgiving… giving to other people to help them during this time of the year. It made me think of an incident that occurred back in the 90's when I was still learning about being interrupted by God.

At that time, I lived in Austin, Texas and I was happily going about my Thanksgiving preparations, running errands and looking forward to time with my family. For some reason I can't remember, I had forgotten to get gas for my car and on Thanksgiving morning, I had run to the convenience store down the road to fill up for the next week.

While I was at the pump, I happened to notice a young woman, looking at her credit card, then the gas pump, and then back to a different credit card…evidently trying to decide about which card to use to put gas in her van.

It was an older van with some rust spots on the fenders and a bumper sticker now torn that read, "my kid is an honor student at". From the look on her face, I could see she had been crying, with red face and tear stains on her cheeks. A faint whine from inside the

van indicated that there were at least two children inside growing impatient. The mother kept saying, "Be patient sweetheart, mommy has to make a decision."

About that time, I had finished fueling my car and was walking into the convenience store to buy some mints and a newspaper. As I walked in, I heard the store attendant say over the speaker at her pump, "Ma'am, the card says "invalid" at my register. I saw panic come over the woman's face, as I walked into the store. While selecting mints, once again I heard the attendant at the register say, "that card says "invalid" too ma'am".

Now it seemed evident to me, this was a woman with a personal crisis going on, and two children in her van. So, as I stepped up to the cashier, I said without a lot of thought, "go ahead and approve that pump for gas and I'll pay for $30.00 of gas for her." The cashier, got on the speaker just as the woman was about to get in her car and said, "Go ahead ma'am, you're approved for $30 of gas, someone just paid for it."

I didn't want to embarrass the woman, and just kind of rushed out the door to jump in my car, but she looked at me as I rushed past and said, "You paid for my gas didn't you?" My face went red and I tried to look away, but she persisted. "Sir? You paid for my gas didn't you?"

I kind of mumbled, "No problem", and was almost to my car, when I saw her break down and begin to weep uncontrollably. Something in my heart broke for her so I stopped in my tracks and walked over to her. I was wrong; there were three children in the car, all of them in child car seats, one of them a toddler. I asked,

"Are you okay ma'am?"

Lifting her eyes from her hands, she looked squarely at me and said, "No, I'm not" She continued, "I am going to a women's shelter, because my husband has been beating me and my children. I found out that my husband removed all of the money out of our accounts so I wouldn't have the money to leave."

She heaved sobs into her hands. I was so clumsy I just stood there as she wept. But she continued, "I was trying to decide with the cash in my pocket whether to get gas or buy breakfast for my son and two girls." I glanced into the van and saw the children were still in their pajamas and one was still asleep in her car seat. I asked her where the shelter was located and she told me in another city, trying to put miles between her and her abuser. Her arms and neck bore the physical bruises of having been roughed up, and at that moment nothing in the world was more important than what was happening right in front of me.

It's funny, how we go about our days, oblivious to the world around us isn't it? I am so self-centered and focused on what concerns ME. This morning was a wakeup call, and if I didn't answer it, I would have been less than human. I must admit, when she placed her head in her hands to sob, I also began to well up.

There is a moment in situations like this, I believe, that God allows us to feel His heart and if we resist it, we become callous, and may never have the privilege of feeling God's heart break again. I'm an extrovert by nature, and am generally a gregarious guy, but something happened inside of me that was other worldly at that moment, and I simply took charge.

"It's okay" I said, trying to calm her down. "You are going to get to where you are going, and "…looking across the interstate, I spied a McDonald's, "we are going to get some breakfast after we fill up your van." At that moment a presence of peace and stillness came over the place where we stood. She even looked at me and said, "Did you feel that?" I shook my head, unable to speak for fear I would breakdown in sobs too.

After pumping gas for her, I said, "Let's go to McDonald's". We all sat down, and her children filled up on hotcakes, sausage, and hashed browns. I couldn't eat a thing, but sipped on a Coke, while she helped her children with napkins and wiping faces. I told her I'd be back and went to a bank machine and got cash for her.

Placing the money in her hand, I said, "I think you can get to ------- (the city) on that. More tears, from both of us this time and as I turned to go, she said, "I had just prayed this morning that if God could hear me, that I needed help... and that's when I heard the attendant say, my gas had been paid for." She concluded, "You were God's answer to my prayer." This time I waited until I got to my car and cried a like a baby. I faintly remembered being used like that a long time ago, and it hurt my heart. At another time, I would not have looked over at her at all, and God would have used someone else... I would have missed out.

I have discovered since that day that doing something, anything for others is what the spirit of Thanksgiving is all about. Every day is thanksgiving when we are willing to be interrupted by God.

Removing the Stinger…

I'm sure I didn't mention it, but a couple of weeks ago, while my business partner Matt and I were tearing out an old deck, we ran into a nest of yellow jackets. One minute there was nothing and the next minute they were everywhere.

I ask you to visualize the following scene two men running away, followed by a horde of vengeful yellowjackets trying to land their stingers. We were slapping our arms, our heads and our pants trying to get the yellow jackets off of us. I'm sure I was yelling, "Get em' off, get em' off!" Matt is a young guy and of course, they didn't sting him once...and then there's me.

I am jumping up and down, slapping my chest, my arms and my legs. Thinking I had escaped, I began to tuck in my shirt again but, around my lower back, right when I was trying to tuck in my shirt...right about the top of my ...ahem...right butt cheek...ZING! I got a sting that made me beat Dwight Stones world high jump record. Oh man...that one little sting hurt all day. Even though it hurt, Matt and I laughed most of the afternoon. I wish I'd had that on video! That was almost two weeks ago. For the past two weeks, I kept wondering why that little sting kept hurting. This morning, back at the scene of the crime...the place where I had been stung really itched. I reached back to scratch it and my finger ran across something SHARP!. I felt again and this time I pinched my fingers over the place where I had felt the sharp object and pulled out a little stinger!!! That thing had been in my butt for almost two weeks. I couldn't believe it!

Of course, while I was using the chop saw, cutting some two by fours the little voice of the Holy Spirit in my head that always makes sense of things, said, "Remember to pull out the stingers or little stings can become infected." Had I been more diligent I would have dug that stinger out the same day. But after days of healing, that stinger worked its way out and then I understood the lesson.

Scripture says, "In the same way, the tongue is a small part of the body, but it boasts of great things.

Consider how small a spark sets a great forest ablaze."

James 3:5

The tongue, just like a stinger can hurt people. I have experience with this. Just like a tiny stinger, hateful or harsh words can sting us, and even days or weeks after the injury, they can still cause us pain. That is why in the atmosphere of tense political debate, we have to find ways to express ourselves that get our point across but doesn't personally attack the person...some of them friends or family. We also have to protect our hearts from being hurt.

I believe we all have the right to express our opinions, and we can do it articulately and with emotional power. I can make my point with memes and with comparisons. But don't expect those who argue with you to use restraint. That is when you have to be sure if they land any stings that hurt you...you need to pull the stinger immediately.

As a proud extrovert, I almost always enter the room mouth first. However, age and experience have taught me that as much as I hate being stung, I too can become a yellowjacket, if I don't watch my heart. Sometimes...(and for an extrovert, that means very few times), it's better to abandon the quarrel.

"The beginning of strife is like letting out water,

So, abandon the quarrel before it breaks out."

Proverbs 17:14

Guard your heart...forgive quickly and chalk it up to fallen human nature.

Arguments, like the sting of a yellow jacket...are a pain in the butt.

Looking In The Mirror...

When we are young, we are beautiful people. We are lithe and fast and strong. We climb, we jump, we run and our bodies are seemingly elastic. I recall doing things, like jumping from a tree limb, scaling a wall, and other things that; if I did them today, would land me in the emergency room. It's just incredible what a young body can do.

And...they look good too! It's why as we grow into adolescents, we look in the mirror so much. The human body in its youthful form is incredibly beautiful. God knew what he was doing when he made us to grow into our youth.

In form, our bodies are strong and long and lean. Young men admire a young woman, and young women stare wantonly at muscular young men. And it's FUN TO LOOK IN THE MIRROR! I told my son Isaac once,

"Dude, really enjoy your strong body, because the older you get, the more your body will limit you; regardless of how much you stay in shape."

He kind of stared at me for a few moments while a smirk formed on his face and laughed and said, "Well, thanks for helping me to look forward to that!" I laughed too...what a wet blanket I was!

A publication I read once did a study about selfies that stated while all age groups take self-pictures known as "selfies", the younger the person, the more the selfies by a significant margin. Although I see plenty of older people placing "selfies" online too.

You've seen it... Youth looks good and they like taking pictures of themselves. If I would have had a cell phone with a great camera on it, I would have taken a bunch of selfies in my youth. I'll be you would have too.

I'm not convinced it is all vanity. You know, I can be as judgmental as the next person, but I want to say that part of the appeal of being young is the ability to attract others and thus propagate the species. Beauty is the attraction of youth. It's the strong suit...the dominant characteristic that unfortunately we define ourselves by in our younger years. Tragically, however, when we are not so lovely according to the fickle crowd in a society that highly prizes beauty, it is too easy to withdraw and judge ourselves as worthless.

Part of the reason the Holy Spirit wants to interrupt our lives is because as we age, we are able to relate to them and share how God has become so central to us as we have aged past those years of youth.

You remember those days...don't you? Maybe you were young, pretty and popular or maybe you were not the "homecoming queen" and less attractive. God wants to use whatever experience you had in your youth to reach the people He brings your way. The question is, "Will you be ready for Him to use you?

Janis Ian in the 1970's wrote THE song that hauntingly tells the story of a girl who understood the value of being young and beautiful called, "At Seventeen".

"I learned the truth at seventeen
That love was meant for beauty queens
And high school girls with clear skinned smiles

Who married young and then retired
The valentines I never knew
The Friday night charades of youth
Were spent on one more beautiful
At seventeen I learned the truth

And those of us with ravaged faces
Lacking in the social graces
Desperately remained at home
Inventing lovers on the phone

Who called to say "Come dance with me"
And murmured vague obscenities
It isn't all it seems
At seventeen..."

In this song, Ian describes the pain of a self-described

"ugly duckling girl" who was deeply affected by not being

able to define herself as beautiful. Her words cut us to the

core, when she says,

"To those of us who knew the pain

Of valentines that never came

And those whose names were never called

When choosing sides for basketball."

As I have grown older, suffice it to say, I look in the mirror less and less. It's because the outward features we fawned over in youth fade in our age. In fact, I believe as we age, we begin to see the REAL person we are… revealed. If we relied on our looks in our youth, but failed to develop the inner person, we discover a void, and an emptiness of character emerges. This is broad brush analysis, and I don't mean to generalize, but what I wish to point out is that, as we age, we begin to discover other, more enduring qualities that perhaps have been hidden beneath the good looks and popularity that are far more interesting and infinitely more attractive than our fading exterior. I passed by the mirror the other day and said, "Hey, what are YOU doing in my house!" It was as if some stranger was staring back at me in the mirror.

We have all heard about "grumpy old people," but I refuse to generalize them just as I refuse to generalize about youth. Not all older people are grumpy. But I DO believe that the reactions of our personalities as we age are either the result of learning wisdom from our experiences in life, or harboring resentment because of them.

From youth and naiveite, we grow to understand about being used by others. We learn during the season of raising children, our own selfishness and if we are submitted to God, we allow Him to change our inner person to one that seeks the best in others. As grow older, we begin to value the contributions of our parents to our lives, and those of others who helped us to mature.

As our children leave the nest, we begin to value our grandchildren and hope to grow into a mentoring role for others. Visits to the mirror become less frequent, and even when we do visit, we no longer admire the reflection for it's attractive qualities. Rather, if; when we look into the mirror there is kindness in the eyes, joy on the face and peace in our brow, it compensates for ANY wrinkle or weight gain. That's because whereas in youth we wear our beauty on the outside, in our older years, the beauty of what inside comes shining through, just as God has designed it.

Also, I have thankfully noticed that the Lord uses me in the lives of young people to encourage and love them. He uses the frailties and mistakes I have made in life to encourage them to do better than I did. It is how redemption works. God takes our biggest messes and uses them like a flashing light to help others avoid the same blunders. The more we expose our frailties; believe it or not, the more useful we become to others. We show the "cracks" in our aging vessels and tell the story of how we got each and every one of them. Let me encourage you to embrace where you are in life. Let others benefit from your life experiences. This is the season of mentoring, the season of elding. We are elders, and we can demonstrate to those younger than us, how God uses "Cracked Pots," like the author of the book of the same name says. I may not look into the mirror much anymore, but I pray that the fractures in my pottery can be useful and show more of Jesus and less of me. Don't hide your

imperfections, use them to show that character developed in youth is what will truly be beautiful later

in life

Hands, Sticking Up Out of The Water…

I used to think I knew what I would do as approached the time in life when one retires…but there is a growing expectancy inside…like something living inside of me that I didn't know was still there. It is rumbling and turning like the ocean…maybe you are feeling it too.

When we are young, we are so busy in our season of life that we don't have time to think too far into the future. We have to go to work, pay bills, buy homes and raise children. But when we age, we still want to do something important, still wanting to make a difference. I often compare present usefulness to past usefulness...which is vanity anyway, because we always overvalue what our contributions were. We blow them up in our minds...we are such pride dogs.

I'm rambling....

As I sat on my patio this evening, I asked God what this gnawing feeling inside of my soul was all about. At first I thought it may just be one of those bullet prayers I pray...just shooting one up to see if He is listening. He was. And, what I heard was both wonderful and terrifying at the same time.

"You had things to do when you were younger...and not much time to listen" he said. He continued,

"You have few things to do now...with all the time in the world to listen...and I think it bothers you Doug".

I sat silently, still listening as Wind In His Hair to the Great Spirit Father as He spoke and feeling angry.

"What you and your brothers like you have to become comfortable with is now listening more than speaking...and parsing your words even when you have opportunity to speak."

I wrinkled my brow, scowling at the ground.

"Oh...you don't like that...?" he asked.

I didn't speak. I've learned to just listen...even when the Lord asks you a question. There is nothing you can say to God that wouldn't be prideful at that moment...He likes to test...He likes it a lot.

"You like to talk...but wisdom WANTS to listen so that when you speak, the words will have weight."

These days I am eyeing retirement and working a little and writing a lot. But in the midst of this world being thrown into a blender and placed in "puree" mode, the word of the Lord looks a lot to me like a bowl of alphabet soup. I can't make heads or tails of it.

But I think from my little talking to tonight, the Lord is taking all of us back to basics. He has taught us (those who came into relationship with Him a while back... in the Jesus Movement) to swim in placid waters.

But now, He wants us to stop showing everyone how well we do the breaststroke and the backstroke, and venture into the deep and give swimming lessons in the midst of hurricanes. There are many who will not make it to shore if they don't have veteran swimmers to help them along.

I'm talking about discipleship…if anyone out there still remembers what that is.

In a dream not long ago, I was in the ocean on the outer edge of a hurricane. The wind would sweep me almost out of the water in a circle. Every time it swept me out to sea, I would see a person's hand sticking up out of the water and I would grab their wrist, and then the wind would sweep me back toward to the shore.

I would drop them off and then, before I could stand up, the wind would sweep me back out to the deep where there was another person's wrist above the water. I would grab them…but just then, on maybe my fourth or fifth trip around in this hurricane, a bolt of lightning lit the sky. When the sky was lit up with the flash of lightning, I couldn't believe my eyes…I saw thousands of wrists and hands, maybe millions, of wrists and hands, sticking up out of the water. I could grab only one at a time…and every time I made the trip, there were fewer and fewer hands sticking up out of the water asking for help.

I began to swallow water and cough, but I wasn't fearful I would drown. The Lord just kept saying, "You learned to swim during a time of peace…but it wasn't so you could show your strokes…it was for this…"

I began to cry out…" Oh Lord…they're all going to drown if you don't sweep others into the storm to help me!" That's when He opened my eyes. Another bolt of lightning crackled and lit up the ocean and there…in the water… were thousands of us…. maybe millions…and everyone had hold of a wrist or a hand, pulling people up from under the water.

When the wind blew me toward the shore this time, I saw hordes of people on the beach…and there were people trying to get them to safety inside. I woke up gasping for air.

As I sat quietly on my patio this evening the Lord said, "You can never tell which end is up in a storm at sea…that is why I walk on water…and as long as you look at me and believe, you won't sink and there will still be work to do no matter how old you are.

The important thing is…it doesn't matter what you and I used to do back in the early days in our relationship with Jesus…what matters is that we remember we learned to swim for others…for the hurricane yet to come.

Gabriella Luciana Vaccarella

I discovered very early in my life, that somehow, God would place remarkable occurrences or people in my very ordinary, unremarkable life. There are no coincidences in our lives. We can tell ourselves that the events that happen in life are just chance happenings, but it is obvious to me that the things that have taken place in my life are by divine design.

At the time they happened, it all looked random of course, but looking back, I see an invisible hand, designing opportunities for that skinny kid so he could draw upon them later in life. It was the year I was a sixth grader at my elementary school St. Bartholomew, that an older classmate named Mike Andress was looking to hand off his paper route to someone. I heard about it from a classmate and asked him if I was old enough to do it.

"You have to have a bike, and you have to pick up your papers and have them thrown by 4:30 before people get home from work". Mike told me.

My brothers and I had all gotten stingray bikes that Christmas so I had a bike but being young and scrawny I couldn't put the bag over my shoulder the way Mike Andress had done. He was the star basketball player at St. B's and was a strong and muscular eighth grader.

I was a skinny 6th grader. After talking it over with my parents, my dad said I could do it, and after fixing a big basket to the front handlebars of my bike, he drove my bike into town and would store it at a local lumber and hardware store where he worked on Jackson St in my hometown.

Every morning, my parents would drive me into town where my dad would let me get my bike out of their warehouse and ride to school about 6 blocks away. As I would ride to school, I would listen to a transistor radio to WCSI the local radio station. I would sing the songs I would hear as I rode, and every day, right after class, I would run down and get my bike off the rack and ride to the newspaper offices to pick up my papers and start my route.

I would throw newspapers on porches, in front of shops, and because I had Route 2A, it was right in the downtown business district in my little hometown. I would take newspapers into to all the stores that lined Washington Street, onto Brown, and Jackson Streets and Fourth Street.

My father gave me permission to enter the Sportsman's Bar which of course was a BAR... but only to place the newspaper on the end of the bar. I delivered newspapers to people up in the apartments that were in the second and third floors of some of the businesses that lined Washington St.

In one such apartment, lived a singular older woman named Mrs. Vaccarella... Gabriella Luciana Vaccarella. On the first day I walked the darkened hallway, illuminated by a couple of lightbulbs hanging from the ceiling and lined with three apartments, I recall Mrs. Vaccarella peeking through a crack in the small door she had barely opened. She looked at me with these piercing brown eyes to size me up. \

"Where's Michael"? she asked with a bit of suspicion.

As I looked in her direction she narrowed the crack in the door opening, not sure who I was. I responded with confidence,

"Ma'am, Mike isn't your paper boy anymore, he gave his route to me"

She looked me over, and probably figured she could take this skinny kid in a fight if I was lying to her and said,

"Okay then… I'm-a gonna have to train you like-a I trained him, so come-a here!" in her thick Italian accent.

She directed with her hand motioning me toward her door.

For a moment her hand disappeared but came back a second later with a paper bag filled with blue ribbons made of silk or nylon and about a quarter inch wide and about six inches long. "These are what you tie my papers with…you roll-a the paper," she made gestures like rolling a newspaper with her hands,

"Then-a you tie them with-a this blue ribbon…capiche?" shaking her head in the affirmative.

Every sentence ended with "capiche?"

"Yes ma'am, I understand", she interrupted me,

"I not-a finished yet!" A look of impatience came over her face.

I stood there blinking and she said, "Don't-a stand there blinking come-a here!" again she motioned with her hand sticking out her slightly open door.

"You then lean-a the paper right-a here…"

pointing to where the door met the door jamb. She could tell by the look on my face I didn't get it. So she took the paper from my hand and said,

"Okay, one-a lesson and only one-a lesson and if-a you don't get it, I'll call-a the newspaper and have a them send a me a new paperboy…capiche?

"I didn't know what capiche meant but I wasn't going to lose my first job because of my linguistic ignorance so I just nodded yes. She took the newspaper and leaned it against the door and closed it.

When the door closed, the paper leaned over right to where the newspaper would fall into the crack of the door when she opened it just a little bit. That way, she wouldn't have to expose herself to any harm by opening the door all the way or having to walk out into the hallway to get it.

The ribbon, well, that was a story for later, but for right now,

"Tie-a the news-a paper with-a the ribbon. Capiche?"

Every day, like clockwork as I climbed the stairs with the two lightbulbs hanging in the hallway, the door to Mrs. Vaccarella's apartment was closed. I would remove the rubber band on her paper and tie a blue ribbon to it and lean it "against-a the door"

As I would turn to leave, I would hear her door open ever so slightly, hear the newspaper falling in and the sound of her door closing with the words.

"Good-a boy, you remember! This-a gonna work out!"

She would later say to me, through the door of course, attempts at humor like,

"You a young-a boy, why you move-a like a me?"

"Speed it up, get-a here faster tomorrow! Capiche?"

We would begin a banter through that door, Mrs. Vaccarella and me. She would ask me about my

school, if I had a pretty little girlfriend,

"If-a my mama and-a papa were Italian. How many-a brothers and a sister did I have? Why she not-a see me at-a St. Bartholomew in-a Mass?"

When it was hot, her hand would pass me a coffee cup with Coca Cola in it through the crack in the door. She would wait for me to drink it and then open her door again to retrieve her cup.

In the winter, she would place a pair of gloves against her door and tell me to "put them on-those boney hands" then she would give me the same cup but this time with hot chocolate. If I would say I couldn't stay, she said,

"Shut up and-a drink it"

She would laugh like a hyena when she got tickled by something I would say, but only one time…only once did she open her door. It was the day I delivered her newspaper for the last time.

I was moving on to Jr. High school and had to give up my route. When I had dropped off her last paper, I called to her behind her door.

"Mrs. Vaccarella, I won't be coming anymore, I have to quit my paper route."

There was silence. I said,

"I'm starting Jr. High school in the fall, and I won't be coming back into town."

I didn't hear any stirring coming from her apartment, and thought, maybe she was asleep.

As I turned to walk away, I heard the faint creak of her door and looked to see she had opened it all the way. She hadn't made a sound, but for the first time I had my first look at Mrs. Vaccarella.

She had a tear trickling down her cheek.

"My little Blue-Ribbon boy…come-a here."

I walked over to her door and for the first time I saw what Mrs. Gabriella Luciana Vaccarella looked like. She was thin with high cheek bones and a very dignified long neck. She had dark circles under her eyes but with full make-up they were only an imagination. Standing with a book in hand, a novel, her frame stood straight…nothing bent over, no trembling even though in the eyes and estimation of a 12-year-old, she was fully 70 years old. She carried herself with an elegance that I had never seen

Her apartment in one of the sparsest buildings in downtown Columbus, was bright and white with lovely furniture in it. A picture that looked like a sunset somewhere in her homeland of Italy hung over her white leather sofa. She looked at me for what seemed like a full minute. I felt as though I was being studied and even; for a moment, I felt she could see right through me.

Then, taking my face in her hands in a caress, she ever so gently slapped my right cheek and spoke in Italian looking into my eyes saying,

"Nella vita c' e dolore, ma na vi e la crescita"

that meant, "In life, there is pain, but there is growth". She smiled at me, and said, "Douglas Pacheco...I'm-a not-a gonna forget that-a name boy! Capiche?" I smiled back and nodded yes, with a lump in my throat.

The door closed. And that was it.

I turned down the hall to finish throwing my newspapers and entered into the summer of 1971. In the spring of 1979, an article was published in my hometown newspaper about me going to South America as a missionary. My time was taken up by raising money for airfare and speaking at area churches. One morning in early May, a letter arrived by mail to my parents' home. It was addressed to me in lovely handwriting. As I opened the letter, out fell a hundred faded blue ribbons and a note that read, "to my blue ribbon paper boy!" with a check for $1,000 signed by Gabriella Luciana

Vaccarella. The God of the Unremarkable had shown up once again.

Lessons in Freedom from Offense

My dearly departed friend <u>Joe</u> <u>Smith</u> once said, "I want to grow to be so free of self, that I don't even recognize when someone insults me."

That is a tall order for anyone but especially for a man of Latin descent as myself. Today a man and his wife came in talking when I walked up behind them. I heard him say,

" These dummies probably don't have high school educations, so let me do the talking."

I laughed inside because I knew it was a test from the Lord. His wife spoke in a beautiful Latin accent, and I immediately knew she was Brazilian.

I lived in Brazil for 5 years as a missionary. The husband said, "We are redoing our shower...it is 3 feet by 5 feet which means...it's how many square feet?" Looking directly at me. I smiled and said..."Let's see, that would be 15 square feet"! He grinned and said,

"That's right!" Good, you might be able to help us...

Without missing a beat, I spoke in Portuguese to his wife and asked, "From which part of Brazil are you?"

She lit up like a Christmas tree and we began speaking in Portuguese.

The husband, wanting to put me in my place said,

" Well, well, let's see if you can tell where I am from".

His accent was pure Castilian Spanish. I could have chosen Spain but instead, because she was from Brazil,

I gambled and said, "Argentina...maybe....Mid

Argentina!"

He stood amazed. He was from the very City I had been to in 1979...Cordoba. I was amazed too! I tried to recall my

Argentine Spanish…and began speaking to him. He blushed…then said,

"I am embarrassed, because I told my wife that you salespeople probably weren't very smart. I told him,

"Sir, because of my God, he has made me wiser than my teachers…it has nothing to do with me. God has taught me through hardship and struggle…and you're right, I only have a high school education. He shook my hand and said, "My sincere apologies for underestimating you". I was not offended…I know without the Lord I would know nothing. Thank you, Jesus, for your goodness. By my God I can run through a troop and by my God I can leap over a wall! Thanks Joe Smith, your teaching continues to bear

fruit!

Decision at the Pump...

We got back from our trip to Indiana this afternoon, and as soon as the luggage was unloaded, I jumped back into my truck to head to the grocery store.

You know how it is when you travel...the pantry wasn't completely bare...but I was looking forward to eating so I figured I needed to stock up for the week.

As soon as I was finished, I went over to the Kroger gas pumps and was going to use my Kroger points for discount gas. I was excited because there were two Kroger cards that

I used in November for groceries, and I was sure that I had at least $0.50 cents off per gallon.

I pulled up to the pump and scanned my first card. To my surprise it still had money on it from October! Between the TWO cards, I was going to save $2.00 per gallon off of my gas! Two cards with $1.00 each!

You may think, "You spent $2,000.00 at Kroger in October and November?!!! No... I hadn't, so I went to the cashier and told her,

"Hey, listen...I have too much money on my Kroger cards...it says I have enough points for $2.00 per gallon off my gas purchase."

She smiled, "No...no mistake," she said after looking at my card and punching in a little code,

"...we doubled your points for being a loyal customer...you can get any amount of that off now and use the rest later if you want!"

I was thrilled! So, back to the pump I went...anticipating the huge amount I was going to save. I drive an eight-cylinder truck...

At that moment, on the other side of the pump, a guy and his wife were talking quietly...and he said,

"Sweetie, we only have $22.00, and this is about the cheapest gas we are going to find…"

I was embarrassed that I heard them talking…I felt I had been eavesdropping, albeit unintentionally. His wife, completely in his corner said,

"Well, let's put it in, and we'll just believe for dinner…you have to get to work tomorrow." There was a little girl in the back seat.

Here was a little family at Christmas time trying to make decisions on how to spend a fixed amount of money…and saying they were going to believe God on how to eat dinner.

I stepped over the divider between our two pumps, and I said,

"Okay…you don't know me…I don't want any arguments, and I don't want you to say anything except thank you Jesus."

I scanned my card and off came 1.00 per gallon off their total. This made (here in Tennessee) their gas cost $1.22 per gallon. I then inserted my debit card and told them,

"Fill it up!"

Now…they were staring at me like I had two heads. The wife didn't cry…she didn't become effusive and begin thanking me.

Instead, she closed her eyes raised her hands right there and just said,

"Jesus….Oh…. Jesus….thank you, Lord God!"

I felt like I was eavesdropping again, and I stepped back over the median to where I was going to begin pumping gas. I could hear them worshipping…and not looking over and trying to do what I had forbidden them to do.

There are times you wish you were just invisible…you know? But I remembered the time my children were that little…and I wondered what I would do at Christmas… it was late December in Tucson, Arizona

1986…and there was a knock at our door.

I opened the door, and there were bags of groceries on the porch…lots of them. Not only groceries but the exact brands we usually purchased. There was no one at the door when I opened the door.

I heard this couple at Kroger get into their vehicle, praising God, and I was just so ecstatic… because I so seldom get to do anything like that. Of course, being the absolute baby that I am, tears came

down my face, and I began to thank the Lord too.

I looked at my Kroger cards, tried to remember which had just been used for the couple, and scanned one of them.

Up on the screen came the message, $1.00 per gallon discount. I wrinkled my forehead and went back to the cashier.

she said,

"Yeah...I just told you we doubled your points..."

I told her I had just used the points for another couple, and she shook her head and said,

"Well, looks like God ain't done yet, honey!"

I wrinkled my forehead, trying to understand what she meant, but she laughed and said,

"Baby, why you gonna question bein' blessed? Does you not want a $1.00 discount? Mr. Kroger mus like you!"

I walked dumbly back to my pump and filled my tank...with Premium Gas for $1.39.

Then I heard the Lord laughing and saying,

'Yeah baby...does you not want to be blessed?" I laughed and then cried some more.

These things don't happen EVER in my life, but one thing I know...There is a God who cares for young families because they are so precious to Him.

He created a memory for them to remember for every Christmas for the rest of their lives...and safeguarded it for His glory by having me admonish them before they got blessed to only give Him the glory...

.."O Come, O come Emmanuel, and rescue Captive

Israel,

that mourns in lonely exile here, Until the Son of God Appears.

Rejoice, Rejoice, Emmanuel, shall come to you Oh

Israel.

The Substance of Things Hoped For...

There is nothing like having confidence in   what God has promised you.

When we KNOW without a doubt that,

come what may, God has complete control, there appears a supreme confidence. Confidence that the big dog is going to take care of everything we have asked of Him.

"This is the confidence which we have [a]before Him, that, if we ask anything according to His will, He hears us. 15 And if we know that He hears us in whatever we ask, we know that we have the requests which we have asked from Him."

I John 5:14-15 NASB

Remember the Song "The Broken Road"? by Rascal

Flatts It illustrates perfectly what I am talking about...

"I set out on a narrow way many years ago
Hoping I would find true love along the broken road
But I got lost a time or two
Wiped my brow and kept pushing' through
I couldn't see how every sign pointed straight to you
Every long-lost dream led me to where you are
Others who broke my heart
They were like northern stars
Pointing me on my way into your loving arms
This much I know is true
That God blessed the broken road
That led me straight to you."

Well, all that to tell you how God moved in a miraculous way.

Twelve years ago, when Mary Ann and I started a winery in my hometown, we decided to sell her car, because we didn't need three vehicles. So, we put up for sale her Toyota Solara.

Mary Ann loves convertibles. She had bought that car, and it was her little treasure. When we sold it, it was just selling a car to me...I mean, you know, people sell cars every day. But as we watched the person who bought it drive away, I turned and, out of the corner of my eye, I saw a little tear in my wife's eyes.

Mary Ann is a silent crier. She makes no noise and doesn't want me to see when she cries...in other words, she's not an ugly crier.

But when I asked her, "Why are you crying?" She said that that car symbolized something to her...freedom maybe, or just that she'd had it for so long that it was a part of her. She said, "maybe someday I can get another one..."

Toyota stopped making Solara's in 2008. There were no more being made. But I prayed "Lord, if at all possible, help me to find another Solara for my Mary

Ann."

Every time I saw one, I asked the person what year it was and asked if they were interested in selling it...the answer was always, "No!"

Years went by, and we bought her a little car (not a convertible) but every time I saw a Solara I talked to the person driving it...and it was like God would not let me forget what I had asked for. Even when YOU are not faithful to remember the prayers you prayed...or when you gave up on them, God didn't! God won't treat you that way.

A week ago, as is my custom, I went to the grocery store, to buy a few things and I came out and placed my groceries in the back of my truck. It was a day like any other day...and Jesus showed up.

A woman putting her cart in the corral, was walking back to her car sitting two cars away from my truck. It was a flawless 2007 Toyota Solara. It was a gorgeous metallic blue.

Now I am a clumsy guy, so, as she was walking past me, I asked, rather stupidly...

"A ma'am, excuse me but how old, " I hesitated for a moment, and she later confessed, "this guy is a weirdo if he asks me how old I am!"

I then quickly finished my sentence..."How old is your Solara?" She broke into a smile, told me what I just wrote above about being a weirdo...then she told me the year.

"Well, it's my mother's and she gave it to me because she doesn't drive it anymore...it is in perfect condition...it's been garaged since she bought it...and we just don't need it!"

My stomach got tight, and I asked,

"Would you like to sell it?"

She almost jumped up and down,

"We would LOVE to sell it!" I took pictures. We agreed on a price. She drove away, and we picked it up on October 5th. It has low mileage and Mary Ann, and I are going on a trip to the Blue Ridge Mountains with the top down in early October.

I thought God had forgotten...but he hadn't! And He won't forget about the desires of your heart either.

Thank you, Lord, for remembering the little things...that mean so much to us here on earth. I love you so much! Thank you for the Broken Road!

On Aisle 12...

This morning, I was at it early again. Removing the first of three full pallets of frozen food and stocking it at my favorite small grocery store. This job was intended to do exactly what it did today...it provided me with a contact...and God with a child of destiny.

I like to listen to books on my earbuds. The company allows me to listen with one earbud in; my other ear is free to hear customers if they need help.

While the book was playing, I had a song going through my mind that I had sung back in 1990 when our church in Austin was joining with other churches to do a march through the city. It was a march begun by Graham Kendrick, a worship leader who had written a song entitled, "Shine Jesus Shine."

It was a simple little song, a bit wordy, but it was a declaration to the powers that be that the church of Jesus Christ was declaring that God owns the earth.

We sang as we marched,

"Lord, the light of Your love is shining
In the midst of the darkness, shining
Jesus, light of the world, shine upon us
Set us free by the truth You now bring us
Shine on me, shine on me
Shine, Jesus, shine, fill this land with the Father's glory
Blaze, Spirit, blaze, set our hearts on fire
Flow, river, flow, flood the nations with grace and mercy
Send forth Your word, Lord, and let there be light"

It was a battle strategy...a call into the darkness that the Army of God was awake...and we were marching. Some onlookers laughed, but it was a shot heard round the world...

This morning, I hadn't thought of any of that, I was just whistling it as I listened to my audio book. I didn't think much of it, I liked the melody, and for some reason, (a notorious phrase for "and as God would have it") it was swirling around in my head.

I was about forearm deep into the French cut green beans when a tap on my back rocked me back into reality, and as I turned to see who was there, I saw a thirty something black woman with piercing blue eyes looking at me and before I could ask "What can I do for you?" she blurted out,

"That song...that is a song that my mother sang as she marched through the streets of Chicago with me in a stroller and about 8 thousand other Christians!"

I smiled and then laughed a little and then told her the story I just told you about Austin Texas. She asked me the words, and I spoke them just about as I posted them up above in the last paragraph, with some of the words different due to my poor memory. She stood there, and her eyes lowered to the ground.

She asked me, "I can't tell you why yet, but may I ask you to sing that to me?"

Well, it has been a while since I sang anything publicly, but I really didn't consider this public because it was just me and her, and I thought she wanted to hear the melody...so I sang the first verse and the chorus.

The woman raised her eyes toward heaven and said,

"Okay mama, I'm coming back!"

The woman... we will call her Cheryl, had lost her mother to a lingering illness not many years after that Chicago walk, but she would sing her daughter to sleep with that song by Graham Kendrick.

As the little girl lay in her bed, her mother would say to her, "Whenever you hear that song Cheryl, it is me...telling you to come back to Jesus." Cheryl said,

"I'll not walk away form jesus Mama!"

But then she said,

" Well, I did...I strayed away from God in my teen years, after my mama had died, and I was involved with a man who left me with two children and disappeared.

"Every day I would pray for God to forgive me for walking away from Him, and I asked the Lord this morning to give me just a little sign that He heard me and still wanted me as his daughter...and then I walked into this store and heard you whistling, "Shine, Jesus

Shine."

I didn't move, and almost couldn't breathe...the presence of the Holy Spirit was right there in Aisle

12... and then she said,

"Those words are God's answer to me...

"Jesus, light of the world, shine upon us

Set us free by the truth You now bring us

Shine on me, shine on me..."

She choked back tears, I could tell, because she couldn't complete her sentences. I was as dumb as a post...I couldn't say anything, it was like God had a sock shoved down my throat, and I was unable to speak. And then she raised her voice and sang fullthroated,

"Shine, Jesus, shine, fill this land with the Father's glory

Blaze, Spirit, blaze, set our hearts on fire

Flow, river, flow, flood the nations with grace and mercy

Send forth Your word, Lord, and let there be light" She sounded like Whitney Houston! I had tears running down my face...the dairy person, stocking dairy came slowly walking around from aisle 11 and was wide-eyed. The entire store went quiet. No buggies, being pushed, no cash registers, just her singing and me with snot running down my nose...

When she finished, I wanted to say, "You sing beautifully," but again, the sock of God was wedged firmly in my mouth…I just stared at her, and then she said,

My mama told me that when I heard that song, it was

HER calling me back to Jesus…and that's why I said,

"Okay mama, I'm coming back!"

Finally, with the power of speech restored to me, I began to thank her, and she gently placed her hand on my mouth and said,

"No… thank YOU…God is filling the nation with His Spirit through people like you…and now, with people like me!"

We spoke for just another minute before she said,

"Pray for me…you must be Christian…pray for me."

And so, I did…I prayed for the latter rain…to fall on this vessel reserved for God's glory. I prayed for her to be filled with the Holy Spirit, I prayed a hedge of protection, I prayed restoration of things that had been lost, I prayed for her ministry…that voice that would awaken the dawn and bless the God who gave

it to her.

I prayed for her to return to church, bound the schemes of the devil over her, and spoke out loud in JESUS name to break every curse that might have come upon her life... I claimed her back for the Lord and declared she was GOD" S PROPERTY!

"She looked up and said, "This was the first time in 30 years that I have heard that song! I'm coming home!

I couldn't speak again, and Cheryl opened her purse and dabbed my eyes with a tissue and then her own. I prophesied over her...and said,

"You are a trumpet in the hand of God, and the Lord will sound your voice over the land and heal it...just like He is healing your heart right now. "

I invited her to church, gave her my email, my wife's email, my Facebook, Twitter, and Instagram accounts;

I think I gave her my shoe size and favorite color too...

She walked away singing and turning around and smiling at me as she walked away...she was singing, "Just As I am..." with that beautiful Whitney voice of hers.

That's when I remembered the second verse of that song...

"Lord, I come to Your awesome presence

From the shadows into Your radiance

By the blood, I may enter Your brightness

Search me, try me, consume all my darkness

Shine on me, shine on me "

There is a wind that is blowing, and it is blowing across all of the dry bones in our land, and it is placing sinews upon them...an exceeding great Army...and this morning, on aisle 12 I saw it fill the lungs of a warrior...and she is alive!

I had almost made a decision to stop writing about these events that happen because I didn't think they were doing anyone any good. I told that to my small group last night...but I'm not quitting after all... His Truth is marching On!

Jesus is not always the Answer....to pain.

I used to be a pastor.
And I am not one any longer. Suffice it to say, there were some areas in my life that closed the door to being able to stand behind a pulpit ever again.

Sounds ominous huh?

There is a very high standard that Jesus has for those who would care for His sheep. His forgiveness is always available, but in my case, I received a pink slip from the Holy Spirit telling me to vacate teaching or preaching to a church body again.

I will share it sometime with you, but it ain't pretty, and there needs to be a good reason to disclose it to you. But I will...one day.

Now that you are speculating in your mind what I could have done to be banished from the pulpit, the Lord DID give me an alternative to it and still be allowed to teach. But it had some conditions to it.

He told me I could write, but the main condition to being able to do so was to never hide the dealings in my life from others.

In other words, when I am going through an area of embarrassing vulnerability, or failure... or a trial in life that I would rather hide... the Lord has told me that it may be painful to disclose it to others, but... if I would be obedient to admit them, He would use them as an encouragement for others who are going through the same kinds of things.

He also promised to give me authority over embarrassment. A promise He has kept by the way.

Now, I am just like you.

Who on earth wants to tell people about your greatest failures on social media where all my followers can read about it and decide you are nothing but a big mess up? Not me.

But here is something I have learned.

Although forgiveness of our sins is promised when we confess and forsake them...Jesus is not always the answer to pain. In fact, He is often the cause of it.

And our pain in life is not always going to be remedied by prayer and laying on of hands.

The author and teacher Larry Crabb says,

"Jesus Christ solves the sin issue—not the pain issue. To follow Jesus is to follow him into the pain, into the dark emotions, into the difficulty. How we ever deceived ourselves into believing that "picking up your cross" could be a solution to pain is perplexing.

Crosses hurt."

So, after having written about how I was having a hard time with my memory on Facebook the other day, I thought I was doing better. I was convinced I was finally "getting" how to do my job. I felt a confidant that I was going to defeat this aging memory thing… …right up to the point where I was fired last week.

Now, I didn't do anything wrong. But I agreed with them, that I just couldn't keep up. There were already 10 clients I was having to make estimates for, and I had 8 pending appointments with new clients.

My work was causing me to get up at 4 am to get a jump on doing estimates and kept me up late in the night. And I was falling behind.

I had to admit that things I could do easily just 10 years ago…I just can't do anymore. And there were no hard feelings…they were very generous with their praise of my hard work and dedication to the company. I left and came home.

Mary Ann knew it was coming too. We had talked about my struggles with computers and the tools for estimating. She met me at the door, and I cried in her arms.

I'm a former collegiate gymnast, I speak three languages fluently, I've traveled to four countries, and I can communicate better than most…and here I was at 64 without an income…terminated.

I was hurting. I would stare off into the distance on our deck. Mary Ann my sweet wife… just touched my hand and would say "Hey" in order to snap me back to the present.

And when I asked the Lord to dull the pain…He very lovingly and graciously said, "No."

And He told me that I needed to embrace it and that in doing so, I would find Him in it.

Dan Allender and Tremper Longman III wisely write,

"Ignoring our emotions is turning our back on reality; listening to our emotions ushers us into reality. And reality is where we meet God."

I tell you all of this for one reason…cause that's my agreement with the Lord.

When we pretend that we are "instantly healed" of the hurtful things that happen in life, we short circuit the very work that God wants to do through it.

It is okay to grieve…and kick the car or the tree or…whatever. God doesn't consider our feeling disappointment of losing our job or a pet…or a child as a lack of faith.

It is why we asked Him to save us.

Life preservers keep us from drowning...but we DO swallow some water.

It is one of the greatest gifts we can give to others because when we admit we are still in pain, it tells people that the church is a place where you are allowed and invited to cry your deepest tears. My favorite author, A.J .Swoboda writes,

"When John describes heaven in the book of

Revelation, he says that heaven will be a place where Jesus will wipe every tear from our eyes. But that implies we enter heaven having been crying. We all need a place to cry. But we also need a place to cry where there are others who might help wipe away the tears. In heaven, someone else wipes away our tears. May it also be in the church. We need a church where we can come and cry."

I wonder, in our efforts at marketing a form of Christianity that appears appealing and victorious to the world if we've created a church culture where we publicly "put ourselves together."

It isn't a place where we can cry anymore. In public, we smile. In private we fall apart. I'll tell you: I've sat in the back and cried in the presence of Jesus. It's liberating. It's life-giving to simply be in the presence of God, who has emotions just like you.Suffering happens, and pain... is not optional.

There are some days that I feel so alone

Now, don't get me wrong, I have a wonderful wife and lots of friends...and wherever I go I always seek to be friendly and make new friends and acquaintances.

But as I was driving this afternoon to the store, I recognized that the two guys I used to be able to call about anything, meaning, my brothers, aren't around anymore. I will hear a song that reminds me of Greg and hear something that reminds me of Geoff and I will get that longing...the deep longing in my soul to feel like I have family around me.

I have a sister who won't talk to me...far away. And then, of course, my parents are gone and are with the Lord. I feel like, maybe God has forgotten about me.

Maybe I haven't done enough...maybe I still have missed the point of my existence on earth and until I get it right, I'm gonna stay right here. I know this isn't true...God doesn't forget us...but I'll bet those of you who have lost family feel that way too at times.

We're the ones who have been left behind... like my wife Mary Ann. She doesn't have to tell me that her two parents are now gone...parted from one another for one earth year, and then they were both just...gone.

I'm sure she feels lonely even with me in the room, although she has her two brothers still here.

As I pondered this today, I arrived at the store where I was driving, and heard the song "Take Me Back" by Andre Crouch and the Disciples. A song I first heard at 16 years old...50 years ago. And, I thought about what good I was down here. I did want to go back...to the place where Jesus was brand new...and have that excitement again. And as I thought about this, I walked into the store.

I was standing in front of the lockers at Home Depot, where I was retrieving some pool cover clips I had purchased on line and was looking at my email for the code to open the lockers, when I heard a little voice behind me and a hand tap me on the shoulder.

I turned to see a woman looking intently at my face and said, "Ray?" "Ray is that you?! I could sense an excitement in her question, and I felt bad that I had to say, "No ma'am, I'm not Ray...I'm Doug." Her shoulders sort of sagged and she said,

"I could have sworn you were my brother Ray...he passed away twelve years ago." I smiled and asked,

"tell me what was so wonderful about Ray."

He eyes looked away and up to the right..."Ray made people happy...he spoke with every stranger and made friends with everyone he met...Ray didn't know a stranger." She smiled at me and said, "I'll bet you are a lot like Ray...aren't you?"

I got a knot in my throat...and couldn't talk right away. I do like to make friends and don't know a stranger... i answered,

"Yes ma'am, yes, I am a lot like Ray." I told her about my thoughts as I was driving to the Home Depot...about feeling alone, about wondering what they all were doing...and feeling envious that I wasn't there to do it with them.

That was when she said the most amazing thing...

"Oh...no. No YOU were left to help the rest of us not feel alone. God left you here because there are some of us who need to see Ray or, whoever they have lost, and God is using you to console us...to be our Ray's and to give us the warm feeling that we have family down here still."

Somehow, I got the locker open and retrieved my pool clips, and when I turned around she was gone... I mean, GONE!

I walked through Home Depot looking for her, up and down every aisle, I went to the parking lot and looked in and at every car in the parking lot... but she had vanished into thin air! No kidding, one second she was there, and the next she was gone! My back had only been turned for a maybe twenty seconds...GONE.

As I walked back to my truck, I shook my head and said, "Lord, that was really strange!" And the Lord said, "Pick up your purpose again Doug...there are people who need to know they are not alone, and the less you think about how alone you are and more about how you can help them know I'm here...you'll not feel like I've forgotten you. My calling is how you know, I haven't forgotten you."

There are things to be done down here...and if you are one of the "last ones" in your family, God wants us to be family for others, and to show that there is a family reunion taking place up there...and we are the ushers directing them to the wedding party.

As I pulled out into traffic, I kid you not, there was a truck driving by...it was a plumber's truck with the name, "Greg and Jeff's Plumbing and Septic service." God never forgets us.

Getting to the heart of the matter...

I walked into the store the other day to pick up something for dinner. I was on my way home and just decided to stop in and grab something. I have to be choosy now, with type 2 diabetes what I eat and how much. Of course, no sugar, no rice, no potatoes no, no, no...

As I walked through the produce department, I was trying to decide if it would be head lettuce or Spring mix, when; out of the corner of my eye, I saw a woman picking up heads of lettuce and then throwing them down...hard!

"Bad Day!" I thought. I continued selecting cucumbers and other greens and again this woman was picking up packages of celery and looking at one and then throwing it down and

picking up another. The force with which she was throwing legumes was disturbing. It was like she wanted to call attention to herself.

A few other customers glanced in her direction, and I saw eyebrows raise and people scurry off to do the rest of their shopping or maybe just to get away from her.

I lingered.

I still needed to find some parsley and for some reason, Publix doesn't place many rolls of plastic produce bags in the department so I was looking for them. As I approached one of the rolls to tear one or two off the roll, this woman was picking up apples.

Yes, she was throwing them down and this time one of them hit the floor. Inwardly I was done with this, and I didn't care what the people around me said. She threw another down on the pile, and it fell on the floor and I just said firmly, "Stop it!"

She looked up angrily at me. I continued, "If you've had a bad day, that's fine, go home and throw things, but stop acting out and tearing up merchandise!" I kept eye contact with her. She was seething, and I could see it wasn't at me. She was angry with someone, and she couldn't control herself. I was bigger than she was and I think she figured I worked there.

I picked up the apple and put it in my cart. It was all torn up and I was going to give it to the produce guy.

She calmed down as she watched me and said, "I'm sorry"...and started to cry. I stayed where I was and certainly wasn't going to touch her in any way, but realized my rebuke had brought her to her senses. She said again,

"I'm sorry...I am just so sorry..." I told her it was okay and then I got a word of knowledge.

I asked her, "something happened at work, didn't it? ..." she interrupted me, "...and the supervisor embarrassed me in front of the entire department!!" Tears ran down her face and I could tell something had really hurt her. I began gathering six apples from the stand where she was standing. I'm not allowed to eat apples with Type 2 but I was buying apples today...if you know what I mean.

Amazingly there was a roll of paper towels sitting nearby on a cart

I grabbed one and handed it to her and she gratefully accepted it.

For some reason, I began telling her of all the times I had been embarrassed publicly. I told her the time I was in Brazil and was speaking in public at church and I inadvertently used the wrong phrase and instead of saying, "I was a chicken" as in I was a coward, I ended up saying the wrong words and in Portuguese the words I said were slang for "I was a street prostitute".

The congregation roared with laughter, and I had never turned that shade of red before. I did that a lot in Brazil...my Portuguese needed a lot of work. she began smiling and started giggling a bit.

I then regaled her with stories from birth about being embarrassed and by the time I was done, she was laughing. Just about then her phone buzzed, and I thought, well, my work is done here and began walking away giving her some privacy.

About 5 minutes passed and I was in the meat section when she approached me and said,

"Sir, I really appreciate you taking the time to talk me down off the ledge today." I laughed and said, "If you want to know the truth, I felt in my heart that the

Lord told me you had been embarrassed at work."

She looked down at her shoes and said, "It made me so angry...I just felt like I did when I was a little girl,

and my mama would embarrass me in front of my friends saying I was the "ugly duckling" of the family.

It was a deep wound, and it would happen again I told her if she didn't get healing for it.

She told me the phone call she had received was from her husband. She had told him about the incident at work and that she was at the store getting groceries. For some reason, he felt she was angry enough on that phone call that he wanted to come to the store to be with her. As if on cue, he walked up to us as we talked.

She introduced her husband to me, and I shook his hand and introduced myself. I finished my thoughts with him present. "When we have been injured as children, we carry that within our hearts, and we react every time someone touches that hurt." A small tear appeared on her cheek again. Her husband placed his arm around his wife and shook his head approvingly.

At that moment, it would not have been appropriate to go into a full inner healing session. (You know, now that I think about it, I think I chickened out...Jesus wouldn't have cared about appropriateness.) At any rate, I told her when she got home to place a chair in front of her and pretend her mama was in that chair and to get it all out of her heart and then to SAY OUT LOUD, "Mama, I forgive you and I love you." (Her mother had passed away 12 years previous.)

As we parted ways, they pushed their cart toward the checkout line and we chatted about churches and I marveled as I looked at them. This couple could have been models...they were beautiful! I realized that the god of this world hates the creation of God and tries with all of his might to destroy them. This lovely woman who was called the "ugly duckling" of the family couldn't have been further from that description than black is from white.

Tonight, when I got home, I saw the six apples I bought sitting on my counter and remembered her. I realize that much of our inner anger is a lack of forgiveness and when someone pushes that button, we go into a rage. The song by Don Henley tells it like it is:

"There are people in your life
Who've come and gone
They let you down
You know they've hurt your pride
You better put it all behind you baby
'Cause life goes on
You keep carryin' that anger It'll eat you up inside baby
I've been trying to get down
To the heart of the matter
But my will gets weak
And my thoughts seem to scatter
But I think it's about forgiveness
Forgiveness"

I forgot to tell you, that the scripture I heard in my heart tonight when I saw those apples in the bowl in my house was,

"Like apples of gold, in settings of silver, is a word spoken in the right circumstances at the right time."

Proverbs 25:11

Aldi is a "Small Box" store

W e had an Aldi open down the road in lovely Nolensville where I used to live.

Nolensville is a small town with zero fast-food joints. Everything is privately owned, the pizzeria, the barbeque place, and the local fried chicken establishment. The grocery stores, however, are all National chains, including Kroger, Publix, and our newest "small box" store Aldi.

Aldi sprang up overnight like a weed in the garden of grocery plants. Their squat stores, with few employees and their ingenious way of keeping their parking lots free of shopping carts or" buggies" as they call them down here, with a simple quarter slot. People would rather die than leave their quarters in the parking lot. Why other "Big Box" grocery chains haven't done this is beyond me…

I began shopping at Aldi years ago when I lived in Northern Kentucky. Their generic aisle markers containing generic cereal brands, generic Rice-a-Roni knockoffs, and good cuts of meat without the really high prices made it a no-brainer when deciding where to shop.

I had to get used to bringing my own bags because at Aldi, they keep prices low by not having the overhead of printed bags. They open the bulk boxes on their shelves, and you grab your coffee out of the box. It's that easy. Even generic wines like Winking Owl (not so good), but they are expanding their selection…

On my birthday this year, I went to Aldi to shop. I keep my head put on right by doing the shopping. Like mowing grass, it is a leisurely stroll; at a grocery store, I can interact with people.

Today I needed some interaction, and a lady named, Yolanda was trying to decide if she had enough money to buy the salmon patties or get some crab cakes in the frozen section.

I don't know Yolanda…I just heard her on her phone telling whoever was on the other side of the call, "This is Yolanda."

Her daughter Renee was sitting in her buggy, pointing at every item on the shelves. Yolanda was doing math in her head… a mother on a budget trying to make ends meet. When I rolled past her, I was making an executive decision about whether Millville cornflakes would be as good as Kellogg's (they're better). I could tell by the items in her buggy that things were tight.

In situations where your heart wants to help, but your brain is telling you that you will offend someone if you offer help, the tug of war becomes intense. My need to communicate for my mental health's sake and the desire to show Jesus' love were at odds with each other.

Do I begin a conversation that surely would be frivolous chatter, or do I remain silent and find a way to help? Always…. ALWAYS help my friends, if you have the ability…and let the chips fall where they may.

Renee kept asking her mommy, "Mama, can I have that?" pointing at canned peaches. Yolanda smiled at her child and said,

"Baby, we can't buy those right now." There are a lot of reasons why people are stretched thin financially. Yolanda stood tall, carrying herself with dignity but possessing a reserved calm on her face. She looked at the hamburger and got the 70/30 instead of the ground sirloin…$1.28 a pound less expensive.

By this time, I was making a Beeline to the front register, and I was in luck. Aldi has begun carrying Aldi gift cards…and in my heart, the music started to play.

I asked the checkout guy to place $100 on the card, and then I swore him to silence. "Dude, don't tell the lady I am giving this to who gave it to her…okay?" He smiled, nodded, and then started checking out another person.

I made another beeline back to where Yolanda was to ensure I could secretly add the card to her cart. She walked away from her buggy, holding her daughter for just a few seconds, and I had time to place it on her buggy where her daughter was sitting.

I kept walking after the drop-off, like a secret agent who had made the microfilm drop. I turned the corner, grabbed my cart, and began pushing it down

the final aisle.

I watched from across the store as she walked back to her cart. At first, I thought she wasn't going to see it. Then, right before placing Renee back in her cart, she looked down and picked it up.

I saw her push her cart to the front of the store and begin to give it to the manager. The checkout guy saw what had happened and said,

"Ma'am, someone bought that for you as a gift." She asked who, and the checkout guy... true to his word, said, "I promised not to tell."

Yolanda began looking around the store suspiciously. I thought, "Oh God, I've offended her!" I put my head down and pretended I was interested in the generic Huggies brand diapers and even picked them up to read about their "snap back" leg to keep from leaking.

I was impressed.

Yolanda was on the prowl...walking around asking people if they had given it to her. I planned my escape by getting in line at the checkout and just whistled...I even grabbed an extra "Aldi" bag for ten cents. I almost made it.

There was a tap on my shoulder. My bladder wanted to empty reflexively. Turning around, I almost did my impression that I did on campus back in the '70s pretending to be Hispanic and saying,

"No comprendo Senora!"

When my eyes met hers, she smiled and said, "Hey man…it had to be you cause there ain't no other person in here looks as guilty as you!"

The checkout guy started laughing, and I whipped my head around to give him the stink eye. Nothing doing…he laughed, and she laughed and said, "You busted, old man!" That made me laugh just to be called "old man" by a stranger in the checkout line at Aldi…that was a first.

She said… no, COMMANDED,

"You get outta that line and come over here!"

At this point, I wasn't sure whether I was in trouble and was going to get put in my place. But she asked my name, and I asked hers. She looked me in the eye, and I couldn't look back. She said,

"You know, I don't know how you knew things were tight, and I don't want to know…but; she squared up and looked at me and said, "God is gonna give this back to you a hundred-fold, because that is Who He is!" I looked at her and said, "I'm paying back a debt

Yolanda."

"Years ago, when my children were little and right around Christmas, there was a knock on my door. When I went to the door, there was no one there, but twelve bags of groceries were sitting on my porch."

That night I remembered crying my eyes out. It was

1986 in Tucson, Arizona. All I knew then was that God sends his angels when we are down. Then, He makes US His messengers and sends us on assignment when we can help others.

We stood talking for a while, and Renee was getting fussy. Yolanda hugged me and said with a tear in her eye,

"This means so much...but especially for my baby..."

Then she turned and went back for the sirloin burger.

Before I left, I could hear Yolanda singing "Joy to the World," and at that moment, I went back in my mind to that little apartment in Tucson, and when I got in my car, I teared up again. This time it wasn't as special

because I was not successful at staying anonymous...We are all brothers and sisters down here...trying to make our way back home. And tonight, you have someone who needs you to pay forward to them what God has done for you.

Will you?

James

Today was a late day going into work. Since I had the morning free, I tried to do some of the errands that needed to be done. That included going to my old haunt Publix to pick up some meds that I needed.

I also picked up a few things Mary Ann asked for. Going early to the grocery store is unfamiliar to me. Empty aisle with store personnel stocking shelves and listening to the background music on the speakers. It was like I had the whole store to myself.

When I finally made it to the pharmacy, I requested my meds and a little voice inside said, "Get some cash." I never carry money...ask Mary Ann. Usually, if I have any cash I will give it to her. Folding money isn't as convenient as swiping a card, but today, I kept feeling I should get some cash.

So, I got $20 bucks and signed for the meds and after a bit more shopping, I drove home, got ready for work, and took off. The 40-minute drive almost always gives me an opportunity to pray.

I'm not very detailed with my prayers! Lord knows, if

He wants something done that's REALLY important, He will give it to someone else. No one wants the world to depend upon my somewhat scattered and incoherent prayers. It's like trying to enjoy music on a record with a skip in it...just change the record!

As I approached the bottom of the ramp to the exit to my place of employment, the light turned red.

To my left, I saw an older man that I determined was in his seventies. He walked bowed, shuffled his feet wearing old oil-stained work shoes. His shock of white hair was further accented by a long white beard. His appearance was unkempt, and, well, dirty. He walked on the median to the left of the off-ramp back to where he had a seat with a sign that rested upon it reading, "GOD BLESS YOU! Veteran U.S.M.C.

The small voice spoke again saying, "Give him the money!" I laughed at having the opportunity to give money to him. Since I never carry money, today I realized for the first time in a while the Lord wanted me to engage again. I thought it was a lot of money though. The Lord reminded me that twenty dollars was worth about five dollars these days and to not be stingy with HIS money.

In the past, I had always had people tell me that giving money to "these people" was just "feeding the curse." That means I suppose that all people asking for a hand were trying to cheat others or that they really didn't want to work and by giving them money, I was perpetuating their ability to collect free money without any accountability.

But since those days, I had dumped that advice in the waste bin. I know that there are SOME who are unwilling to work and sit around all day asking for money. I hadn't always given to "panhandlers" before due to this seemingly sage admonition.

In fact, I never recall hearing Jesus say, "Do not give to the poor, because you will just be feeding the curse." No. He never said that. Some tell me that giving "them" money is a waste of God's resources..."They'll just buy liquor or drugs with it! they say. but even though Jesus said, "You will always have the poor with you, but you will not always have me here with you!" It's God's will to bless, it is His will to love, and these days, when time and traffic will not wait, money fills the bill...(no pun intended!)

I knew in my heart, just like I knew in the grocery store when I got the extra money, that these incidents were a God set up. He's so good at this stuff.

"I called out to him, "Hey! Devil Dog!" (That's the designation for a Marine). He turned slowly, with a smile. He limped over to my truck as I handed him the money. He took my hand as he received the gift.

"Thank you, thank you so much!" He grinned showing a full set of pearly whites. I asked him where he served and he said, "Okinawa, 1972-76!" I smiled and told him my son Josiah had served in the Marines in

Okinawa as well. I told him about my son Isaac and my daughter-in-law Jessica...Marines all. This is when he smiled broadly and said "The last person that stopped and gave me money had prayed with me and said, "Someone today is going to give you $20 dollars!" Opening his hand he looked at the bill and realized it was that exact amount.

Tears streamed down his face. The light had turned green and before I left, he looked at me and said, "It's been a hard few years for me...but today you gave to the Lord...and God will repay!"

I drove off for the last ten or fifteen blocks, but before I got too far, I looked in my rearview mirror and saw him wiping tears from his eyes. I thought about James (that was his name) all afternoon while I was at work.

As I drove home, I pulled out of our company parking lot and headed toward the interstate. As I got close to the on-ramp I looked to my right and there, painted

on a wall with spray paint were the words once again..."He who gives to the poor lends to the Lord, and God will repay!"

Of course, we must discern the opportunities that are presented to us during our days, but the one thing I know is this...I would rather err on the side of mercy when standing before the Lord and giving an account for my life than to trust some lame "don't feed the curse crap. Help the poor, feed the hungry, clothe the naked, heal the sick, raise the dead.

The Gospel of the Kingdom is the power of God to meet his wayward children even on the highways and byways. He tests us to see if we will listen and obey, and He Himself may be the person sitting at the offramp that you pull up to next.

"And the King will reply, 'Truly I tell you, whatever you did for one of the least of these brothers of Mine, you did for Me.' ." Matthew 25:40

Mercy Is a Sword

I had just turned left onto Concord Road off of Nolensville Pike when, from a distance, I saw the car pulled over on the shoulder of the road.

I was late for work because I had made what I call a "drive-thru" cup of coffee, meaning a travel cup filled with coffee from my home coffee pot.

For those who don't know, "Drive-Thru" coffee is one of the staples of balanced spiritual people. Some other staples include pop tarts, chicken and biscuits, and large quantities of chocolate milk. These ,along with fried bacon and donuts ,are essential to make one wise.

I mention these things just in case anyone was wondering what contributes to my acute spiritual acumen.

Sipping on my very hot coffee with cream and enough sugar to stunt the growth of anything good in my body, I, of course, rubberneck (the art of slowing down to stick one's nose in the business of anyone unfortunate enough to be pulled over on the side of the road, yet making sure you don't inconvenience yourself by stopping to help), to see what misfortune had befallen the motorist.

I was in luck! I was able to see that the car evidently had a flat tire. Thinking to myself, "What a pity," all the while thanking God it wasn't me, I consoled myself with the thought, "Oh...that person is close to all kinds of businesses or gas stations...they'll get the help they need."

I patted myself on the back for slowing down to show I cared, then drove on down the road.

The drone of my tires against the concrete roadway and the music streaming through my truck speakers were not enough to drown out the inner voice trying to tell me to stop, turn around and help.

Coming to my defense, my right hand turned up the music as Timothy Schmitt of the Eagles sang, "I Can't

Tell You Why" and I sang louder too.

Reaching for my perfectly balanced coffee, I tried lifting it by the lid, and the lid came off...coffee spilling all over my spiritually balanced front carpeting and partially ruining my chicken and biscuits.

Praise did not emanate from my pie hole.

I was ticked off that I had done something so stupid. And just as I had pulled over to sop up the creamy, sugary mess out my driver's side window, I saw people rubbernecking ME! That's when the inner donut voice said, "How's that feel?" "How does it feel to need help and people just pass by?"

Rebuking Satan and continuing to clean my carpet, I had to get out of my nice comfortable truck cab to walk over to the other side of my truck to get some shop towels out of my back seat to finish cleaning up the mess. Again, out of the corner of my eye, I saw people slowing down to look at my misfortune, only to gun it when I made eye contact.

I realized at that moment that, as a driver, looking at someone on the side of the road and saying 'Bummer" did not help them at all.

In fact, It was at that exact moment that I wouldn't have given a rip about how good someone prayed for me if I had really needed some help...and then, I remembered the person with the flat tire.

"No," I said out loud.

"I am not the archangel of roadside repair...life happens, and that sometimes stinks!" I said to no one standing there.

This soliloquy happened in three seconds. I busily wadded up the soaked paper towels and threw them in my truck bed under some cardboard so they wouldn't fly away. Getting back into the driver's seat, I looked into the rearview mirror to make sure no one was nearby when I pulled back into the road.

As I looked, I realized that all the spilling and cleaning and inner voice resisting had taken place only about 50 yards past the person with the flat tire.

I sat looking at that car in my rear-view mirror for almost a minute.

This was a pivotal moment.

Did you know that dread almost always precedes me moving in obedience? Yes, DREAD. It's because serving others is not convenient and not a natural impulse. Self-sacrifice

...crawling up on the altar, and willingly laying down our lives... quite simply sucks.

There, I said it. Having mercy has to cost you something, and oh, how my flesh hates it. The greater the mercy, the higher its value impacts a life. Believe it or not, I NEVER considered whether this would make a good story at that moment! I usually try running from stories far more than I ever live them!

My eyelids closed, and then I looked forlornly at my empty silver "Drive-Thru" coffee cup from my formerly favorite big box store. I then remembered something I wrote last summer.

"Inconvenience is one of God's greatest servants." "Crap!" I thought to myself.

This means that nine out of ten times, whenever I have to do something that requires self-sacrifice, it is usually God's Spirit saying,

"What are you going to do?" I then have a choice.

Going against the direction of traffic, I reluctantly backed up closer to the car with the flat tire. Again looking in the rear-view mirror and making sure it was safe to get out of my truck, I opened the door and walked toward the person sitting in the car. I waved and stood back so they would know I was safe and shouted,

"Are you okay?" The guy in the car rolled down his window and said,

"Yeah, I'm good!" I was relieved.... I thought to myself, "

Hey, I said to myself, "He's good...I can leave!"

My natural inclination would have been to say,

"Okay, man...just checking!"

My conscience assuaged, I could now walk away with confidence knowing I had listened and obeyed. Only I didn't say, "Okay, man...just checking!" No. Instead of escaping, my mouth opened again...against my will. "You have a jack? Is someone on their way?"

The guy looked miffed. "No, but I don't need your help," he yelled back.

I scrunched my face into that "What do you mean?" look and walked closer to his window. Did I hear him correctly? I asked him,

"Did you say no, you don't have a jack, and no one is coming?" He nodded in the affirmative. He didn't have his phone in his hand, so I wondered what I should do. Not knowing where my jack was located on my truck (it's under the back seat, I discovered), I again walked closer and asked,

"What are you going to do?" He scowled at me. "I said I don't need your help!

I shook my head to indicate I understood. I then realized that he DID have a spare and that he DID have a jack...but he didn't know how to change his tire! He was about thirty years old. I felt an inner nudge and said,

"Hey, I'm all dressed in construction clothes; it doesn't matter if I get dirty...want me to get your jack and tire out of your trunk?" It looked like he sighed like,

"Oh man, I don't need the humiliation of you discovering I don't know how to change my tire." Without waiting for him to answer, I said,

"Pop your trunk!" and began walking to the rear of his car.

The trunk popped open. He then got out of his car and walked back to where I was in order to see what I was doing.

"Man, you don't have to do this...I can figure this out!" he said in an agitated way. I nodded without making eye contact.

"I know you can…so I'll just get it out and set it up and let you do it…that way, you don't get all dirty." I then chanced a look at him. His hands were on his hips, and he said,

"Oh, THAT'S where the jack is!"

I tried to make a joke, saying that carmakers tried to hide the jack from car owners, and finally got a little chuckle out of him.

I set up the jack and his little "donut" tire next to the car's side.

He wanted to save face…I could tell because, in all honesty, he didn't know how to use or where to use the jack. I just continued looking for the lift point near the rear tire for the jack, placed it under, and began to lift the back of the car.

"Is the emergency brake on?" I asked. He looked at me and said,

"Oh, yeah, I guess that's a good idea."

During all this, I continued loosening the lug nuts and lifting the car. He was taking mental notes. Again, he said,

"You didn't have to stop…I could have figured this out!"

I smiled…and the voice inside said,

"Mercy is gentle…be gentle."

"I know you could have," I said as I removed the flat

tire.

This was when I realized that being shown mercy for the lost is embarrassing and frightening because it exposes their need for it.

For those who live in this world who believe they are the captains of their own souls, the Fruits of the Holy Spirit are a threat to them.

I continued silently without acknowledging the guy at all. I replaced the flat in his trunk and placed his jack and tire tools in the trunk as well. I wiped my hands on my jeans.

I didn't offer my hand to shake or say, "There you go!" I just began walking back to my truck.

The guy was silent until I was almost to my truck. He then used the last weapon he had in his arsenal to save

face...

"Hey man, I can pay you…hold on!" I swiveled and shouted,

"Stop…wait a minute!"

I walked back toward him so he wouldn't reach into his car to get money.

I finally said it out loud.

"Okay, I don't want your money…just like you didn't want my help."

That slammed the door on that. He stood looking vulnerable. I said,

"You may not want to hear this, but God saw you on the side of the road this morning and had someone stop to help to show you He is There and Real. That is the only reason I stopped…THE ONLY reason I stopped."

The guy blinked and looked directly at me. "I don't believe in God," he said. Unshaken, I said,

"I know that…that's why you were shown mercy…God will never stop showing you He cares until you finally give up and acknowledge Him or slam the door forever!"

I was surprised by the force with which I said it. I turned around and walked back toward my truck.

Getting back into the cab, I looked in the rear-view mirror to check the road and merge into traffic. My truck smelled like dark roast with cream and sugar. I felt no compunction, no urge to read him the "Four Spiritual laws" or give him a Bible or my email or blog

site.

That would have lessened the point.

The Fruits of the Holy Spirit are lethal firepower to pride, arrogance, and self-sufficiency. They are the assassins of the lie that "You are the captain of your own fate."

Love, joy, peace, patience, kindness, goodness, faithfulness, gentleness, and self-control are the tangible evidence of Christian morality still alive in the world, and they kick pagan philosophy in its fat backside!

The Fruits of the Holy Spirit is the aroma of a country that the lost do not know. Their presence on the earth is both enticing and heightens their senses to the fact that there is a land they do not know or understand...and it scares them.

God gives a slide show to the inhabitants of the earth on the screen of His people...if they are willing to be inconvenienced.

We belong to a country far away, Whose King is loving and compassionate, and we speak a language that is foreign to the inhabitants of this earth.

We are ambassadors of a Sovereign who bids us crawl upon the altar of sacrifice in order to demonstrate what his Kingdom is all about.

Take up your cross...show the passport of your citizenship to that faraway Kingdom and show the earth that Jesus is still looking for them...Still looking.

Abusers Need Healing and God Uses Us to Do It...

I learned this the other day while at work at my favorite big box store.

I am a people pleaser, which means that I try hard to make sure people get what they

want.

In this case, as I stood in my department stocking the faux wood blinds, I was approached by a lady who was visibly agitated. I looked at her and said,

"Hi, you look frustrated...what can I do for you?"

She was dressed professionally, wearing a tailored suit with black heels and her nails manicured. Her hair was raven black, and she held her shoulders back (good posture) as she walked toward me. I smiled...she didn't.

"First of all you can get that sh*t-eating grin off your face and stop what you are doing...I've been here 5 minutes and no one has helped me!"

She continued,

"You people (I'm not sure which people she was talking about) just stock your d*mn shelves and don't give a sh*t about customers!"

At this moment I was still trying to understand what it was about my grin that was bothersome and trying to imagine why one would grin after eating the substance she mentioned. My mind finally caught up and I tried to apologize for her inconvenience, but she would not have it.

"Don't talk..." she shouted, looking at my name on my apron.

"Doug...don't give me your pathetic little excuses...DOUG" she said condescendingly.

"What I want, DOUG…" she pointed her finger and punched it at my name on my apron, "is for you get you're a** up on a ladder and get down two of those

G-D tubs that are out of stock!"

Let me take a moment to explain that the line between allowing a person to vent their frustration in order to decompress (which is healthy and full of grace) and/or giving them permission to stomp on you because they are a bully, is in my humble opinion, determined by how much emotional control and maturity you possess.

That decision cannot be made at the moment of conflict. It must be determined far in advance…in other words, you must know what your boundaries are going to be before it ever happens. Your response… if you possess your soul, is not retaliatory…it is not a reaction…it is a responsible line that you have predetermined.

She stood scowling at me. I looked down at my shoes. There was a time in my past life when I would have given her a piece of my mind and taken it as a challenge to see if I could wither her self-confidence with my own cruelty. At a former time in life, I had been good at it! This time,

I asked her to please walk me to the area so I could scan the item and see if it was still in stock.

Her anger did not abate. She began to say,

"Some of us who have REAL jobs, AND lives, don't have time to wait for you!"

At this time, I was pushing the ladder toward the tubs where she had been pointing so I could climb up to retrieve the tubs. I had to be careful because there was another woman with a child in the aisle. The professionally dressed woman again spoke up and said,

"Let's get this done today, DOUG!"

I climbed the ladder and retrieved the two tubs. She did not have a cart and so I said,

"I'll go get you a cart for this ma'am." She blurted,

"I don't have time for that…carry them up to the front!"

To be a Christian does not mean we lay down on the ground to allow the world to walk on us.

I don't believe in doormat Christianity.

I believe that we are an aroma of life to those who are being saved and we are an aroma of death to those who are perishing. At this point, I was approaching the limit of my own self-control. I began to carry these up front when the woman said, "Let's pick it DOUG!"

I stopped and placed the tubs on the ground. Like

Joyce Rachelle says in her book, "The Language of

Angels",

"Woe to him who offends a patient man who has just reached his limit."

I said,

"I have been nothing but accommodating to you today…and you have done NOTHING but speak

abusively to me, cursing and trying to bully me like I am sure you bully everyone else. But this is as far as I go…pick them up, and take them yourself!"

Her face contorted into an angry form and before she could speak, I said,

"Don't…summon your soul and just DON'T! I am a human being just like you and I will not be treated this way. If you don't like it,

THERE is customer service and of course you know my name by now!"

She looked into my eyes, and I saw tears forming in hers.

I hadn't spoken but maybe 50 words...but I had drawn the line. She shook...kind of convulsed. Her hands formed into little fists, and I thought she was going to hit me...or attempt to.

A tear trickled down her face... she gritted her teeth and said,

"I apologize."

Her harsh demeanor turned to a sorrowful almost heaving but silent cry. Her only words were...

" going... hard , going through a...divorce."

There is always a reason why people act the way they do...and this woman saw me as the outlet for the pain and anger she felt at that moment and decided to treat me the way she had felt treated.

She kept trying to communicate..." not your fault" ...my fault...my fault". It is unlike me not to try to console, but I stood ramrod straight and waited for her to look at me. She calmed herself.

I didn't feel particularly loving or compassionate I'm sorry to say. But I DID still hear the Holy Spirit say,

"Pray for her."

I admit right here and now that I wanted him to pick someone else to pray. I didn't want to do it...I didn't like her; I didn't care one way or the other what her situation was.

I am being painfully honest. But every single stinking time I get into a deal like this, God always says I have to be an adult and every single time I resent it. Which is why...I'm sure, he continues to do it.

I placed my hand on her shoulder and prayed.

"Lord, please give grace to my friend (I choked on that word), and grant her peace to accept the truth that you oversee our lives. This Christmas make her gift... a confidence in Your ability to see her future...that it is good and filled with hope."

I didn't wait for anything. I picked up the tubs and walked them to a cashier. She was fishing in her purse for tissues.

Without saying goodbye, I turned to walk back to my department. I heard her say, very quietly as I walked away, "Merry Christmas Doug."

When I got back to my department, I was still stinging from being so harshly treated. That's when Jesus, who, after all... this is his birthday month, said,

"They pulled my beard out and blinded me with thorns through my head...and while hanging I asked for them to be forgiven."

Those words went deep into me, but I said,

"But, Jesus, I'm not you...I just am some dumb sinner here on earth and I have a hard time when someone treats me with disrespect. "I'm sorry.

It was a few moments trying to get my soul under control when I went back to stocking blinds. I heard the Lord say,

"I heal the brokenhearted...let me heal yours".

That broke me. I felt all the anger and pent-up rage I wanted to unleash on that woman drain right out of my feet.

I love Christmas...and the spirit of Christmas is joy to the world, peace to men of goodwill, and love toward all who are unlovely...especially me.

The Breakfast Nazi

Whenever I travel, I'm more of a "throw the bag in the car and go" kind of guy. Plans? Overrated. Adventure, I figure, comes from leaving room for surprises. But on one trip back to Northern Kentucky for a family reunion, that philosophy landed me in the middle of the strangest hotel breakfast I've ever witnessed.

I checked into a budget motel — the kind that had already cycled through three owners and a couple of name changes. As the day manager handed me my key, she leaned in and whispered, "If you can avoid it...don't have breakfast here."

"Why not?" I asked. She glanced around, lowered her voice, and started, "It's not the food, it's—" but another employee walked in, and she stopped cold. "Enjoy your stay," she said, sliding me my room card.

Curiosity forgotten, I had a great evening with my kids and grandkids. The next morning showered and hungry, I wandered down to the breakfast room. And it looked perfect: eggs, sausage, biscuits and gravy, fruit, muffins, even a waffle maker. A small oasis of free food. That's when I remembered her warning — about ten seconds too late.

From the back kitchen came a voice that could peel paint. "Who spilled apple juice in the drip tray?!" A woman stormed out, glaring at four burly highway workers. One sheepishly nodded. She lit into them: "Rude! That's just rude! Do you know how much work you've caused me?!"

The men shrank into their seats like schoolboys.

Then she turned to another guest. "One omelet! One per person!" She marched over, snatched an extra omelet off the woman's plate with a plastic fork, and stalked away.

Next, she blocked a man in a wheelchair: "Oh no, you're not holding up the line. Sit down! I'll get it." To an elderly couple: "Haven't you already had two cups of coffee?" To another guest: "Did you throw a cup in the trash with coffee still in it? DID YOU?!"

She actually dug through the garbage, poured three drops of coffee into her sink, and muttered about people trying to kill her.

The "Breakfast Nazi" had arrived.

The room froze. No one dared touch the salt shakers. That's when my mischievous streak took over.

I grabbed the coffee carafe and started table-hopping like a waiter. "GOOD MORNING! HOW ABOUT A WARM-UP?!"

People snickered. I tossed a banana to a teenager, who caught it like we were in a ballgame. I grabbed two omelets and delivered them to the lady who'd been robbed.

The Nazi twitched.

"Boy," one of the guests said through clenched teeth, "You're about to get your ass whooped."

By then, the room was alive with laughter. The road crew applauded. A woman asked for more coffee, and I filled her cup until it spilled. The man in the wheelchair wheeled over to the fruit bar, laughing so hard he touched every piece of fruit twice.

The Breakfast Nazi finally screamed, "YOU! STOP THAT RIGHT NOW!"

But it was too late. The day manager walked in, grinning ear to ear. Guests clapped. I leaned close and told the Nazi,

"Don't you ever forget: people are the reason you have a job. Don't ever talk to them like that again."

She thought I was management.

"Yes, sir," she mumbled.

The day manager later confided, "That was the best thing I've ever seen." She comped my room down to $99 and, by the end of the day, the Breakfast Nazi was out of a job.

Not all interruptions are holy moments — but this one, at least, came with free coffee refills.

Quick to Hear...SLOW to Speak...

If you know me at all, you may remember that I   used to have a quick temper. I came by it honestly. I admit that even we Latins can be controlled by the Holy Spirit, but I'm gonna tell you that we are hot-blooded people! Provoke us to your doom!

However, when the Holy Spirit takes control...we can be even quiet when God directs us to be. And so, begins my story...

I was stocking frozen food, and; as it turns out, Jimmy Dean Meat Lovers and Sausage and Egg skillet breakfasts appear to be the favorites.

One man, the other day, emptied the freezer of both. 25 frozen sausage and egg and Meat lovers breakfast skillets unceremoniously dumped into his "buggy"

(shopping cart for the Northerners.)

I looked at his cart and said nothing. I just groaned because I had just filled the freezer, and now, two big holes yawned before me on frozen aisle 12.

As he walked by me, he evidently had seen me looking as he emptied the contents of the Jimmy Dean section and made a remark to me...

"Dat's yur job!...Go fill it up again!" He apparently was from Chicago. He reminded me of that guy on the movie, "Casino", telling Joe Pesci to "Go get your shoeshine box!"

He stopped directly behind me, waiting for me to make a comment. This guy was a fighter...I could tell and wanted to coax me into an argument. There are many people these days with a chip on their shoulder wanting someone to fight with, and I don't have the time to mix it up with someone over Jimmy Dean.

I turned around and looked at his face. He was around my age... little mustache, but only around 5'4" tall. His attitude was trying to compensate for his short stature I thought.

I smiled.

You LIKE Jimmy Dean huh?!"

His reply was a like out of movie...

" So what are you...a brain surgeon?!"

I laughed out loud, and this completely disarmed him.

I said,

"Let me get you something!"

I walked up to customer service to retrieve two courtesy tickets to give to him, then walked back to the freezer where he had gotten his stash of JD skillets. I got two others I thought he would like and then walked them up to him with the tickets in my hand.

"You might want to try these...people say they really like them. Try them on me!" I handed him the complimentary tickets.

This time, he wanted to make sure I was insulted, and he said,

"You ain't my personal shopper! Go ---- yourself!"

I was unsure I could do as he asked...seeing as it would require me to be a contortionist. But a boldness came on me that is uncharacteristic of me. I wasn't mad, OR insulted...but I looked at him and said,

"Bless you, my friend!" smiled ear to ear and walked back to continue stocking Tombstone Frozen Pizza.

In case you don't know it, kindness is a killer to anger and insults.

He stood there with nothing to say. Little did I know his wife was also in the store, and she had heard his comment to me as I walked away. An argument ensued.

I kept my nose in the freezer because I just knew this hot head would try swinging at me if I gave any indication that I enjoyed his wife chewing him out. I admit it...until I understood what his situation was, I was thinking the guy needed someone to put him in his place...

I felt a tap on my back. I looked around to see if I could use a frozen loaf of Pepperidge Farm Garlic Bread to hit him with if I had to.

It was his wife.

"Sir, I want to apologize. My husband has Aspergers Syndrome." I had heard of it and had previous experiences with someone with Aspergers.

I told her it was not a problem, but I could tell she was very embarrassed. I told her not to be. She had asked him if he REALLY wanted 25 of the same Jimmy Dean skillets and he had said no. she wanted to go and place them back in the freezer.

I told her not a problem...I would do it.

Asperger's or ASD as it is now called, is more frequent in children, but many adults deal with the effects of ASD as well which include,

Repetitive behaviors.

Engaging in repetitive behavior is a common symptom of ASD. This may include doing the same thing every morning before work, spinning something a certain number of times, or opening a door a certain way. Just because you engage in this type of behavior does not mean that you have AS — other disorders can result in these behaviors, as well.

Inability to understand emotional issues.

People with AS may have difficulties interpreting social or emotional issues, such as grief or frustration. Nonliteral problems — that is, things that cannot be seen — may evade your logical ways of thinking.

First-person focus.

Adults with AS may struggle to see the world from another person's perspective. You may have a hard time reacting to actions, words, and behaviors with empathy or concern.

Exaggerated emotional response.

While not always intentional, adults with AS may struggle to cope with emotional situations, feelings of frustration, or changes in patterns. This may lead to emotional outbursts.

As I walked the cart of Jimmy Dean back to the freezer, I stopped and thought about how necessary it is to be led by the Holy Spirit and not react to people in difficult situations.

God calls us to be peacemakers...and being slow to anger can give grace to others when we don't understand their situations.

It would have been just another day on aisle 12 had this situation not occurred, so I thanked God for His restraint.

No sooner had I restocked them; another customer came and put six of them in their cart.

Jimmy gives me fits!

The Fruit of The Spirit...

I went yesterday to pick up some meds at the drugstore down the road. I don't like going into pharmacies, and I usually pick up in the drive through, but this pharmacy closed their drive through, and I am forced to go in.

I had arrived about ten minutes before they went to lunch and I could tell they didn't want to wait on me, but they did. As I stepped up to give them the necessary information, another woman came up and stood behind me in line.

I could see the pharmacy techs and pharmacists roll their eyes. they wanted to get to lunch...and I don't blame them...they are on their feet all day...literally. So, when she came up, the pharmacy tech said, "I'm sorry ma'am, we close at 1:30 for lunch!"

She was older...well, older than me. And I could see her shoulders drop when they said this to her.

"I just need my husband's meds...for his protocol... he needs them right away."

The pharmacy tech was adamant.

"Well, I'm sorry but we've all been here since seven this morning...we will be back in thirty minutes."

I had a lot of meds to pick up...but I asked the tech if she could please make an exception. Another tech in the back said,

"Thirty minutes isn't going to kill someone...if we wait on you, then someone else will come in and we will never get to lunch."

I stepped back and told them to wait on her and I would go and sit in my car for 30 minutes.

She thanked me and stepped up to get her husband's meds. I headed for the front door to sit in the car and wait. I thought,

"Maybe I can go over to the grocery store and get some things before coming back."

I got in my car and started it up, and was trying to get my Bluetooth to sync with my car radio... and there was a "tap, tap, tap" on my window.

It was the lady behind me. I rolled down the window and she thanked me. Her husband had Myasthenia Gravis...they were older...and his condition had worsened over time. I prayed for her and as I finished, out came the pharmacist.

She stood there while I prayed, and then, when I was finished, she said,

"Come back in... I have your meds ready."

I thanked her and said my goodbyes to the lady. She patted my hand, and I shook it. It wasn't a big deal...no lives were saved.

I walked in and the screen had been pulled across the pharmacy counter and the signs were up saying we'll be back in thirty minutes.

I gave her my date of birth and my name, she retrieved my meds, I paid for them and walked away. It took minutes to give her the info, pay and walk away.

There was no trumpet...no angelic visitation. But as I walked into the parking lot, the Pharmacy tech who had told her to wait was driving out of the parking lot and shot me a dirty look.

I thought, "Isn't it interesting that showing kindness to others gets people angry?" Kindness is sometimes inconvenient to others, but if we allow them to cancel out the fruit of the Spirit, then what have we got to offer others?

The trip to the pharmacy reminded me there are multiple reasons we run errands throughout the day. We may think it is to pick up a quart of milk or buy bread...but we are sent on missions sometimes, just to answer a prayer of someone who...that very morning thought they were all alone.

We are sent into work to love the closet alcoholic, to show kindness to the desperate husband, or wife, to give assistance or support to the person who may be thinking of taking their life.

If we don't move in the fruits of the Spirit, then no door can be opened by the Lord to help others. The fruit of the Spirit is the supernatural door opener, to walk into someone else's life and love them like Jesus.

You are the hands and feet of Jesus on the earth, and you will never know how your love, joy, peace, patience, kindness, goodness, faithfulness, gentleness and self-control will touch another's life.

What Do We Do....What Do We Do?

I am an extrovert...for those of you who like people who enter a room mouth first...an EXTROVERT! This means that sitting alone in a room filled with file cabinets and boxes of unfiled papers is the quickest way to a grave for me.

As I am a writer, I write constantly...sometimes online, sometimes for books, and other times articles for magazines. I like to write, but too much solitude can cause me heartburn...and I begin to get depressed.

So, this season of my life, I have decided to go take on a part-time job. This is due to callouses growing on my backside and because I need to be out among people to keep up meeting people...which is the caffeine that fuels my desire to interact with the "Povo"

(Portuguese for People.)

So I have decided to work at a grocery store this time. Yes, that is where I meet most people I talk about in my books. I already worked for my favorite big box home hardware store and figured that I could meet approximately 50-60 people a day if I stand in the produce aisle and tell people not to squeeze the melons or Roma tomatoes. Stories will ensue...no doubt.

On my first day of interviewing, I went into my now favorite Grocery Store, (no... I'm not telling you which one...) and I immediately got confirmation that this is where I needed to be at least 20 hours a week. I can still write a LOT for the rest of the week.

The moment I walked in, I helped two customers find the coffee, and another lady saw me answering questions and asked me where the restrooms were.

The manager was watching and said,

"Oh...you're a customer service guy huh?"

I smiled and asked,

"Is there any other kind?" He laughed, pushed out his hand to shake and he told me where the office was and who to ask for in the back.

There were around 12 employees between me and the office. A woman named Imelda, (not Marcos). I stopped and spoke with each one...just because they were standing there.

Each one welcomed me before I was even hired. One of the people in Dairy stopped me, pointed to an old guy sweeping the floor, and told me, "Don't talk to him...that's Gus...He hates his job, this store, and anyone that gets in his way."

I smiled...and asked, "Why does he hate his job?" Gus was about my height, with deep furrows on his forehead from scowling. He looked in my direction right after the person in Dairy told me to steer clear.

He looked miffed...that someone was pointing him out. I began walking toward him and stopped to check the price of the heavy cream, (Keto don't ya know?), and then kept walking to the end of the aisle where he tried staring a hole into me.

Now...a few things went through my mind, because; of course, I wasn't yet an employee...in fact, I wouldn't even be officially hired until about an hour later. The first thing I thought was typical of me...

"Well crap...Lord, let me explain, I came to find people to encourage... maybe you didn't understand."

The second thing that went through my mind was,

"Lonely and Useless."

The final thing that went through my mind was the

Lord saying,

"You don't need to explain anything to me...I DID understand Spanky!"

(I hate it when He calls me Spanky!)

Walking up to Gus, I saw his inked sleeves, (that's tattoo lingo), and his wedding ring...bigger than mine...(which has revolving lights on it and gives off a siren just so everyone in the tri-State area will know I am married.) It weighs around 50 lbs.

Lol...my wife reminds me that I was the one that picked out my ring.

As I arrived at where he stood, I had nothin'.

I first just thought about walking around him and going straight to the back room to the office the manager had mentioned. But then the Lord spoke up and said,

"Lonely and Useless." And so...I told a fib... not a big one, just...you know...a holy fib. (I keep hoping that's a thing,) I said,

"Hi there, are you Gus?"

Gus scowled, his upper lip pursed, and his eyes narrowed. His first words were,

"Who wants to know?"

I didn't answer, I just said, " I was told you know the store better than anyone and would be able to walk me around and show me how it is laid out."

His face softened. I never grovel when people look angry at me and I never broke eye contact with him, but I DID smile. I added,

I'm new Gus and need some help learning where everything is."

Gus walked his broom over to the hallway and leaned it against the wall. He made some low guttural sounds in his throat, and then, cleared his throat and said,

"Sure, follow me."

We walked and Gus gave me the entire tour. He showed me where the shipping and receiving dock was, He showed me the cardboard bailer, where cardboard boxes are crushed and bailed together.

He showed me the back stock, the ice cream cooler, the dairy cooler, and the large freezer. He walked me to the break room and showed me where magazines and books were on a rack, and said,

"I really like these books!" pointing to Stephen Covey books, who is one of my favorite authors. He said,

"People bring in books all the time...kind of a lending library, where employees can read them and bring them back".

I told him Covey was one of my favorites and he perked up a bit.

Gus then said something that made my ears perk up.

"I read a lot since my wife passed two years ago."

I couldn't say anything after I heard that...because I understood what "Lonely" meant. I told him I was sorry.

Gus had not scowled since I had introduced myself to him. As we walked, I understood what his wife's death had done to him.

He said, "I pretty much lost my desire to do anything." he said,

"I used to be a contractor, but I just didn't want to build houses anymore...I sold my business and paid off my house then sold it. I renovated a little house south of town and banked the rest of the money. I came to work here about six months after my wife passed.

They had met when they were around 20. He had left a vocational school, and she was a teacher. They had no children. He said every day since she passed, he wondered why God left HIM alive but took her.

He asked about me...who I was, wife, kids? Why did I come to THIS store? He asked me what kind of books I liked, and what my hobbies were. I told him I wrote books, and my background was in sales and customer service, and ministry.

I barely mentioned the ministry.

That word has some connotations to it that I'm not crazy about. It makes me think of Bril-creme and ugly brown suits and ties, and the Doxology and pencilnecked preachers and their wives with big hair. I hate brown!

Gus looked at me like he was studying me to see if he wanted to trust me to say something. But he didn't have to...I spoke up.

"Gus, I'm just going to take the chance to say, that you are not useless, and you don't have to go around life being lonely."

Before he could speak, I continued,

"The knowledge that you have as a builder is immense..." and then I said it...then bit my lower lip like "I hope you don't hit me!"

"Your wife would hate that you don't use your

building talent any longer...I'll bet she loved that about you...you could do any "honey do" she wanted!" Then I smiled.

Instead of hitting me, Gus smiled for the first time deep. The furrows on his forehead disappeared and he laughed as if he remembered.

"She DID!" he exclaimed...with a force that almost made me flinch.

"Every time she asked me to do something she just marveled that I could do it, re-wire a house, paint, build a new stairway..." then he said, looking up,

"Yeah, she loved that!"

We were joined in the back storage room by the manager, who saw us talking and was surprised Gus was talking to me.

"Everything okay back here?' he asked cautiously.

Gus spoke up while slapping me HARD on the back,

"Oh yeah...me and old Dougie boy were just gettin' to know each other."

Gus went on his way and the manager had me do some paperwork. I thought maybe I should visit a chiropractor after Gus had slapped me on the back.

My ears were ringing.

He said, "How in the WORLD did you get into a conversation with old Gus? He doesn't talk to anyone!"

I said, "Well, I fibbed and told him you wanted him to show me the store since he probably knew it better than anyone." Sorry.

He laughed and said, "Well, it wasn't a fib...I came back to see if Gus would take you around the store and show you the departments and how the store was laid out."

In my head, I thought I heard,

"I told you SPANKY!" I rolled my eyes.

I finished the paperwork and spoke to the cashiers, the deli people, the boys getting the carts in the parking lot... basically, EVERYONE. They all welcomed me and as I walked out the front door, there was Gus. He was looking at his phone and said,

"What do you think about this little house on the east side? it's a dump isn't it!?" I agreed. Then Gus said,

"I was thinkin' maybe I could go back to do a little bit of house flippin'." I told him I thought that was great and as I walked away, he said, "I think my wife would like that too.!"

In the 70's song "Alone Again, Naturally," Gilbert

O'Sullivan sings,

"It seems to me that there are more hearts broken in the world that can't be mended...left unattended...what do we do? What do we do?"

Jesus came to heal the brokenhearted. Our God is a good God...and He sets captives free. He knows what to do to heal those broken hearts.

And it doesn't involve Bril-creme or brown suits...

thank God!

When God Goes Fishing

I've been pretty silent for a while, not writing   much due to moving into our new home.

There are lots of things to keep us busy, from painting, tiling and moving around the furniture just to amuse ourselves. From time to time, Mary Ann asks me to move the sofa just so she knows I can still do it.

She's a good wife.

However, late August has brought about a new rhythm of its own. I have succumbed to the desire to change my scenery and have returned to working with my partner Matt at our home renovation biz. Matt says good help is hard to find and he said it out loud within earshot, so I am guessing he is hinting to me to get busy and hang that drywall! Fare thee well favorite big box store!

Today however, I had just arrived at the Williamson County Dump and Recycle Center to throw out a bunch of old drywall and carpet we had pulled up from a customer's home. These places are convenient. Not only can you throw away old paint, tires and worn out batteries, but they have several compactors that will crush trash, metal and even a trailer for old mattresses.

I'm telling you this is trash-o-rama!

Williamson County residents can take one full truck load a day...A DAY mind you and it is all paid for in your handy dandy 9.75% sales tax.

Tennessee has no state tax, which is great, but it still feels like passing a peach pit at the register—hard, sharp, and nothing you'd want to go through twice. "9.75% on EVERY SINGLE PURCHASE!

However...I digress.

Today while dumping lots of garbage into the compactor, a younger couple in their mid to late twenties stood on the opposite side of the compactor and were throwing their trash into the dumpster as well. They were young...and in love...Ahhh Youth! And they were quite proud of the fact that he had just bought her a diamond the size of Rhode Island as an engagement ring. She was all of 80 pounds soaking wet and without a doubt she was bigger than he was. She was flashing that piece of ice for all of us trash people to see. In all honesty, she should have been walking with an armed guard. It was beautiful

and...well...

She was thrusting out her left hand for the people on my side of the trash compactor to see when two things happened exactly at the same time.

The compactor was full, Buford, the compactor operator was too busy looking at her ring when he pushed the yellow button that started the compactor moving forward. The thing was full to the brim with all kinds of goodies... 2x4's, banana peels, some rotten eggs, some used baby diapers, (Cruisers...on sale 150 pack for 12.99) oil filters, two or three rolls of fiberglass, an old floor lamp, a box of broken fluorescent bulbs and bags and bags of trash. The second thing that happened was that her ring went flying off into the trash compactor!

It slipped in between some oil filters and believe it or not, I heard it hit the bottom of the steel compactor floor. The thing was mauling and had already begun to break some boxes and bags open…one of them exploded with a "splash" as it went everywhere. The young woman looked horrified and screamed. Buford pushed the emergency stop but things were mashed in so tight after some fretting and crying …and that was Buford doing the fretting and crying, there was NO WAY to reverse the compactor.

Everything ground to a halt and six of us stood staring at the compactor. The woman's fiancé was mad…which; considering that a diamond the size of a softball had just gone into a trash compactor, I guess made sense. Two people drove off and me, Buford the woman and her redfaced fiancé stood there looking.

What to do…what to do?

I asked her if I could pray and she said, "Anything, do anything!!! I want my ring! So, I did. "Lord, I ask you to protect that ring and not let it get crushed." She ordered Buford to start the compactor which, now had a line of cars waiting to dump things into it. Buford pushed the button. The sound of crunching, creaking, splitting wood and squishy garbage being compacted was sickening to hear. I kept hoping that thing was insured.

After the piston returned to it's starting spot, I asked

Buford to turn off the compactor for a moment. Yes...into the dumpster I dove; feet first however...let's not get crazy. Buford handed me his flashlight and I scoured the bottom of that dumpster. I got a sick feeling that didn't come from the used diaper material on the side of the dumpster. I thought,

"Oh no Lord, her ring..." and then...

Out of the corner of my eye, there, right up against a bunch of garbage and eggshells, gleamed her diamond ring...perfectly intact!

I reached down, asked Buford if he had a rag and to my surprise, he handed me an alcohol wipe. I gave it a

quick once over. THERE WAS NOT A SINGLE

SCRATCH ON THE GOLD NOR WAS THE BAND EVEN BENT!

I handed the ring over to the woman and she shrieked with joy! They asked me if I wanted money as a reward. I told her, as I climbed out of the dumpster the only thing that came to my mind…and believe me, I wasn't trying to be spiritual.

I said, "Store up for yourself riches in heaven where the thief cannot steal nor moth destroy…you can do that for me!"

They helped me out of the dumpster and she confided that she had been a lapsed Catholic for twelve years. "but " she said, "I have to go and confess my sins." Being a former Catholic myself, I told her, "God is available right now…you don't have to go to the confessional." She teared up and told me God could never forgive her. Her fiancé stood stone-cold silent as she told me she had aborted a baby and could never be forgiven for that. That's when Buford became my "mighty man of God". Buford pulled out a Bible from a stack of three on his shelf he had pulled out of the trash from various people. He underlined the Scriptures for her and was very bold.

"Darlin' this man has jumped into a dumpster for you but dat don't mean nuthin' compared to whut Jesus dun fer ya. He ain't hangin' on no crucifix…Jesus is

Alive pumpkin….ALIVE I tell you!" Without asking,

Buford put up the "This lane closed" sign and told her

"Jesus "dun come to the trash bin today to find you!".

My eyes teared up. So did hers and her fiancé's. Ole Buford prayed for her and her man. I told her God forgives everything and right there…in the compactor aisle number #2 at the Williamson County Recycling

Center,

The woman and her fiancé prayed the sinner's prayer. Buford, BOLD man of faith, who knew why he was there, he put his hand in the devil's face and pushed him out of the way. In all honesty, no preacher in thirty years has had that kind of anointing on him. He was the preacher, I just got to be there.

After giving them a tract from his church, we prayed again, and they went their way. Buford winked at me and said, "Hey my man, we dun did team ministry and I don't even know yore name!" I gave Buford a big hug and said, "Not important Buford, but thank you for your boldness and authority!" Buford smiled and

said,

"The minute you spoke Scripture to dat couple, I knowed dat God decided to go fishin' in the dump today…you were the hook and the bait…and I got to reel them in!"

There is nothing God won't do to reach people. Be ready to jump into a dumpster. You never know what is going to happen. Thank God. Being the hook and bait never felt so good!

God Uses Even the Tiny Things...in Secret.

When I was young and very inexperienced in the things of God,

I went as a missionary to South America.

Although I spoke Spanish, the language of Brazil is Portuguese. Both are romance languages, and both require a good ear to be able to learn and speak them.

At 20 years of age, I took this leap of faith because I wanted to be used by God somehow on the earth.

My Portuguese was really bad. I mean, folks, both me and the lead pastor would preach on Sundays, but most of the time, when I would teach, there was a lot of laughter in the congregation because I just didn't speak Portuguese very well.

I even took lessons in Portuguese from a tutor and though I improved, the fact is, I'm not sure if anything

I ever taught stuck with those young beautiful Brazilians.

Around two years into living in Rio de Janeiro, my wife and I felt we should go to Brazil's largest city, Sao Paulo to start a church at the University of Sao Paulo.

We found with the help of the other pastors and a Brazilian attorney, a beautiful house with an auditorium with a 200-seat auditorium attached!!! It was just amazing.

You know, we often think that because other people can do something that we should be able to do using faith and a lot of hope to get it done.

We did do a lot of outreaches, but try as I may, I couldn't seem to grow the church very large. It is kind of discouraging when you put all you have into something and only the first two rows are filled in a room of sixty rows of chairs! But God added some wonderful people and nearing the four-year mark, I began to question whether I was supposed to return home.

I went into a fast for three days. My heart was discouraged and quite honestly, I had decided to return to the States with my tail between my legs. I just asked God to please use me...somehow to reach Brazil with the Gospel. I wept feeling I was such a failure.

Do you know what it's like to feel you have failed God in the very thing He called you to do? I wanted to crawl into a hole and die.

I had rented a piano for the auditorium and after fasting for three days, I just randomly went and sat and began plinking and trying to worship.

I had taken about 3 months of piano lessons in third grade but had thrown in the towel...I wasn't patient enough at that age...oh well.

At that time, I remember this melody came into my heart and it was pretty. I played the melody on the piano, put some words to it, and at the next church meeting, I introduced the song.

Both Brazilian churches that the other Pastors and I had founded sang the song. In December of 1984 I returned home to the United States.

I was somewhat disappointed for leaving without much to show but, I needed to move on to somewhere I could be more effective.

A decade and a half later, I received from one of the members of that Brazilian church a phone call.

Out of the blue.

It was Pastor's Day in Brazil, and he wanted to thank me for being his pastor at one point in his life. I was

SO humbled. I had done NOTHING, not even

preached very well.

That was when he said, "But Douglas, you wrote Alpha and Omega!" (The name of the little song from fasting)

I chuckled..." Yeah, well," I said, one little song for four years work...that's not a very good return on investment!" That is when my friend stopped me.

"Douglas... don't you know? Your song has gone all over Brazil...it has reached churches thousands of miles away! God has used it during our revival!"

I stood frozen in disbelief! That little song? That little plinking after three days of fasting? He bid me goodbye, and I was so grateful. I hadn't placed my name on it, hadn't copyrighted it...but it didn't matter.

God knew who wrote it.

A few months ago, our friends <u>Bill Bennot</u> and <u>Connie Bennot</u> went to dinner with us in Columbia Tennessee.

At the end of our meal I distinctly heard women speaking Portuguese. Now I always get excited when I hear Portuguese...

I got up...walked to the table and greeted them in

Portuguese. They were happy someone spoke in

Portuguese to them.

They asked how I learned it and I told them about my four and a half years in Brazil. I said

"I wasn't there very long but IDID write a song..." I added,

"You probably have never heard it!"

One woman named <u>Lara Da Luz Richard</u> said, "Sing

a little of it..."

Embarrassed I began singing...but then I stopped because all four of them began singing it!

I went home and wept. Almost 40 years later these young, lovely Brazilian women were singing a song that was God's answer to my prayer. These women weren't even born when I wrote it!

God is faithful my friends...even if you don't think He is. The smallest thing I ever did, God used to prove to me that sometimes, God answers our prayers later

than we wish, but better than we could ever imagine!

He is indeed...the Alpha and Omega!

Praying For A Headache...

I work going in and out of freezers that are -10 and stock grocery store freezers.

This is what I do to stay busy. I interface with people daily, but lately, I have found myself rarely talking to anyone. This is totally contrary to my very nature. I may have become less garrulous in my older age, but, going in and out of a -10 freezer makes me focus on getting the job done quickly.

I am not complaining. I love what I do because it is useful and a service. I sure don't do it for the money...

Monday, I was busy loading my cart with frozen food, from Marie Callender to Healthy Choice to Jimmy Dean breakfasts. I was loading some frozen pizzas when I happened to feel my right knee begin to throb.

In 2015 I had the meniscus partially removed from my right knee because I had torn it running the Flying Pig Marathon in Cincinnati in 2008. It tends to act up a bit when I walk a lot and has pretty much kept me from running.

As the throb grew in intensity, I began to limp, and it was generally a miserable morning. Nevertheless, I went back into the -10 freezer to gather more frozen dinners and went back out to load up the freezers in aisle 12. Potatoes, fish, and chicken tenders are in aisle

11.

As I was loading these freezers, I glanced over at a coworker who is rubbing her temples. It was clear she has a headache and or some stress causing her head to hurt. So, I don't think about my knee; I just kind of limp over and ask her if she is alright.

"Oh, I'm sure I'll be fine," she said, opening another box of product to stock, "but I feel a migraine coming on, and I don't want to have to go home and lay down...I need the money."

I admired her truthfulness. She had to continue to work in order to care for her husband who was disabled. She is a personable individual and very kind.

She does her job tirelessly and without complaint.

Today is the first time I have ever heard her lament.

I asked her about medication and how she deals with migraines, and she gave me a prescription drug name that I forget. She had run out of that medication but could go to another store that has a pharmacy and pick some up, but she was out of money.

She asked about my limp, and I told her what I just told you. I knew I had to get back to my Banquet Chicken Pot Pies before they began to thaw, and I asked her if she would allow me to pray.

In Tennessee, there may be someone who won't let you pray for them, but I have not run into them yet. She nodded, and I placed my hand on her head. I prayed in the name of Jesus, and she thanked me. I limped away and went back to Green Giant and Birdseye. My knee continued to throb. I also looked up and said,

"By the way Lord, how about my knee? I could really use healing here." I finished my load of frozen food bricks and went back into the freezer to get more. As I passed this woman in the back stock room, she smiled at me and said, "My headache is completely gone!" I smiled and said I was so glad. She thanked me again and asked about my knee.

I said, "I'm almost done for the day and will go home and put my old knee brace on it." She looked a little puzzled.

"How is it that you prayed for my headache to go away, but you still have a bum knee?" I smiled at her and said,

"I asked the Lord the same thing...but I think I need someone to pray for me because it still hurts."

She was shy but whispered, "If you go into the walk-in freezer and close the door, I will pray for your knee." I asked why go into a -10 below freezer...why not pray right here?"

She blushed and said, "I would be embarrassed if anyone saw me."

I didn't judge her...but into the backroom came the manager, and she walked away in a hurry. I finished my day and started toward the front when she saw me limping toward the time clock.

As I went out the front door, my knee continued to throb, and behind me, I heard a voice.

"Hey, stop right there!" I turned and saw her walking quickly toward me. When she got to my truck, she

said,

"That was pretty ungrateful of me to get healed of a headache and then to be embarrassed to pray for you."

Without another word, she prayed something like,

"God, this guy prayed for my headache, and it went away...I appreciate that! Thank you. So, will you please heal his knee?" I don't pray often, so I am going to end this now, this is Jenny, and I am asking you in

Jesus' name. Amen.

My knee stopped throbbing, and I began to laugh. She asked what was so funny, and I said, "Well, my knee stopped throbbing...and there is no ache in it."

She looked at me in wonder and asked, "Really?" I nodded, and she told me she had never prayed for anyone and had not been to church in years...but that she wants to begin to go back. She was flustered and

said,

"I didn't know God would listen to me since I have not been in His house in years." I told her that God didn't heal me because of church attendance; He healed me because she used the name of Jesus."

She turned to go, and I heard her say, "I didn't know God still healed people these days... and He listened to ME?!"

When people begin to discover that Christianity isn't obeying rules, or just going into a church building...when they discover that God will listen to THEM, that He honors His Word above His Name... they will begin to do what this lady did.

The last words I heard her say when she was walking away was, "Do you still remember me, Lord?" "That was Awesome!"

Something tells me she had more of a conversation with the Lord that day than she'd had in ten years...

Does it shock you that God used someone who had quit going to church to pray for me in Jesus' name, and He healed me? What else is God waiting to do for those who seek Him, to show them that He loves them, has never forgotten them and honors His Word?

Beeping Molly...

O kay...So I got out served, out smiled,   and outflanked at the grocery store...
by a little 5-foot nothin' woman named Molly.

So, there I was, dutifully obeying my wife by going to the grocery store and taking a list that was longer than Jacob Marley's chains in A Christmas Carol.

Walking into the store, I always have my head on a swivel...you never know who is going to walk by and skin your rumpus with a buggy (shopping cart for my Northern brethren... 'NO NINOS EN LA CANASTA for my Spanish speaking audience.) So, you must be quick, you have to be agile, and you have to have catlike reflexes like a ninja.

Fortunately, I have all of those... plus I was wearing my "Hey dudes," and I was also looking good! (no

brag...just fact!)

And, as it so happened, I brought my A-game today. This means that if people are looking lost, I can nose up to them and ask, "Whatchu lookin' fer?" and they will tell me, and I will help.

However, today, I was absolutely outflanked by a fivefoot nuthin' lady that I came to know as Molly.

As I looked over the Marlyesque list, my wife gave me, this little dynamo sidled up next to me and asked me,

"Whatcha lookin' fer?"

This was a unique thing for me...and I had to actually fight a voice in my head saying,

"You don't need any help...just tell her you're thinking." Old Proud as a Peacock Doug Pacheco wouldn't take any help! And I looked at her, and as if she could read my mind, she said,

"Now, I've seen you helpin' other people...so just humble yerself and tell me what yer a lookin' fer! We all need help!"

I smiled, turned a little red, and said,

"Okay, I need to find cans of Pumpkin." Molly went into action. She left her cart right there and said,

'I know... aisle 7!" And off she went. I followed her, saying, "Oh, you don't have to go there; I can do it!"

Pride doesn't like to be shown anything...God help me!

As I followed her, I kept hearing a "beep, beep" and thought to myself, "someone has an electric buggy in here..." but I followed on.

When we got to the pumpkin, she pointed and said,

"Right down there!" I said thanks, and she said, "Okay, we're one for one now...I helped one, and you helped one!" And off she walked.

I helped a woman get two cans of some french style green beans she couldn't reach and helped another woman bend down to get some sugar. When I passed Molly, she was up to six and told me so.

I got six...how about you?' I told her I only had three total. She smiled and said, "You gotta look for

'em...you gotta look for 'em!"

I was staring again at my list, and Molly asked, "what is it now?" I mean, it hadn't been 30 seconds since our last little conversation, and I said,

"Those fried Onion things..."

She pulled my cart behind her and led me right to them. I kept hearing a "beep, beep, beep beep!" As she walked me there. I thought she was getting text messages or something.

Finally, Molly helped me find the Coconut cream.

"Not the coconut milk," I emphasized, "The Creme of Coconut!" She turned and looked at me and said,

"I know what you meant...it's on Aisle 3!" And away she walked.

Yes...we found it right there. Molly ended with a score of 13 to my measly 3. I laughed and announced the winner. I was absolutely flabbergasted. she had her cart full and had helped 13 people!!! I thanked her profusely and got in line to check out.

Today was one of those rare days when Kroger had almost every aisle open with actual people checking out the groceries.

I was talking to my checker when she looked behind me and said,

"Hey, Molly!"

I asked her how she knew her, and she told me that Molly came into the store almost daily to do some shopping for her neighbors and friends.

I kept hearing the "beep" and asked my checker what that sound was, and that is when I found out the amazing truth.

Molly was legally blind...and her glasses had sensors in them that were hooked up to her hearing aids and her phone and would beep when something was crossing in front of her or if there was an impediment in her way as she walked!

I had been helped by a legally blind woman!!!

I went up to Molly in the next checkout lane, gave her a big hug, and told her how much I appreciated her.

She smiled, got a little red, and said, "You're welcome...I appreciate your help too!'

Walking to my truck, I felt like the Lord said,

"There is always another encourager around to teach us how to encourage others...you just met one of my best!"

Molly was led by the Spirit of God and a high-tech gadget, and I learned that we can deny others the pleasure of serving us if we are too proud to receive

it...

Thanks, Molly!

Matt...

I went shopping for an updated sound system for my truck. Since I have owned my 2010 Ford F-150 Super Crew XLT I have done quite a bit of work on it, including recently installing a brand new 5.4 Liter long block 8-cylinder engine.

It was cheaper than buying a newer truck since used trucks are selling for a premium these days. With new tires, a rebuilt transmission and some other improvements, an updated radio was just an added improvement that I thought would help.

I ran into a well-known electronics retailer trying my best to dodge the raindrops pouring down in sheets in Brentwood

Tennessee. Upon entering, I found my way back to the car stereo area and began browsing.

Of course, help being a rare commodity, I began looking for someone to answer some questions. One of the receiving crew paged someone, but it took a long time. I thought about coming back on another day; when, around the corner came a young man named Matt.

Matt, wearing a mask, still smiled so widely that his mask practically slid off his face. Matt shook my hand, placed his left hand on my back and said, "How can I help you bud?"

Now, nothing about this was out of the ordinary, except one thing...Matt, besides being extremely outgoing also had Downs Syndrome. I told him I was looking for a touch screen replacement for my F-150 radio. His eyes stared at the ceiling for a moment while

I was explaining what I needed and then, he asked,

"What year is the vehicle?"

I answered and he immediately asked me, "two or four-wheel drive? XL or XLT, or is it a Lariat or King

Ranch?" Now I grinned from ear to ear and said,

"XLT Two-wheel drive!"

Faster than I could walk, he hurried over to the computer and asked, "Does your radio look like this?" He pointed to the exact radio in my 11-year-old truck.

Now I just giggled out loud. "Yup…that's it Matt!"

At that moment another employee came up to us and said, rather abruptly,

"I'll take it from here Matt!"

I didn't like his tone. Matt coward back and I saw all the confidence drain from his face.

You'll forgive me if I got a little P.O.ed at the guy and

I said,

"Matt is helping me just fine!" with my best "You're a jerk!" look on my face.

The recent arrival said, "Well, I'm a salesman and he is still in training, and besides, he can't answer any of your questions!"

I asked Matt to stand aside for a moment while I talked to this "expert". I said,

"I have an XLT 2010 F-150…Super Crew…what radio do you recommend?" "He looked at me and knew I was not happy and said,

"Well, if you just hold your horses I will go and look!"

I took a chance...a REAL GAMBLE because Matt had been so quick to ask all the right questions and I said, "Hey Mr. Salesman...before you leave...I just want to ask Matt the same question..."Matt, what radio do I need?"

I mean without even blinking...Matt said,

"I recommend the Sony XAV-AX 5600...it is a Double DIN In-Dash MP3/USB (GPS Navigation) Car Stereo

Receiver with a 6.95" Capacitive Touchscreen

Display,55W x 4 Channel MAX with 3 Sets of 5V

Preamp Outputs and is Compatible with Apple

CarPlay & Android Auto!"

Mr. Salesman's mouth dropped open...literally. I smiled, and said,

"Matt will take it from here!

Matt's countenance beamed and I said,

"Okay Matt, let's go see this thing!"

He showed it to me, and he said,

"And... it's on sale for 50% off!"

Just then, as God would have it, the Big Manager came around the corner to make sure someone had taken care of me.

I said, "Matt is so good!" "He took care of everything, found me exactly the right stereo, and I couldn't be in better hands!"

The manager smiled from ear to ear and said,

"Matt has a special gift...he has a memory that is almost photographic!" Mr. Salesman tried to butt in..."I was just going to write it up for this gentleman!"

I couldn't help myself. I said,

"Listen if you don't mind, I'd like Matt to finish helping me!" I'm sure there is some kind of commission on sales and the manager simply said, "Sure...Matt, take care of this gentleman and if you need any help on the computer, just page one of us!"

Matt then showed me all the connections, the new radio facing I would need for the truck. He began reciting OUT OF HIS MEMORY the part numbers of

all the parts!

I heard Mr. Salesman complaining as the manager whisked him away and was "giving him a talking to."

We finished and Matt looked at me. He wanted to thank me, I could tell, and I wouldn't let him. Instead,

I told Matt,

"I have been in some type of sales for over 40 years Matt, and I have NEVER had anyone be this exact, confident and professional! Don't ever let anyone try to step in front of you when you are with a customer!"

Matt smiled...shook my hand and said, "Thank you...your installation is included!" He gave me a date for installation which was over a month away, but I would have waited a year for that installation.

The gifts and calling of God are irrevocable.

Before I left, there were two men looking around in the same department for a car stereo. I asked them,

"What kind of car and year of vehicle do you have?

They answered me, and Matt piped up,

"That will be a Pioneer AVH-120BT Multimedia

DVD Receiver with 6.2 Inch WVGA Touchscreen

Display and Built-in Bluetooth© for Hands-free

Calling & Audio Playback | Double Din!"

"If you will step over here, I will take care of you and show you all of the features." I began laughing to myself and Matt caught a glimpse of me smiling.

He looked at me...and merely said, "People judge books by their covers all the time...why should it be any different from judging people?"

He continued, "I started here stocking the shelves, but the manager thought helping customers was a better use of my time!"

"For promotion does not come from the East or the West or from the desert. but promotion comes from the Lord...he lifts one up and abases the other." Psalm

75 6-7

Never Ashamed...

I was shopping quite a few years ago in a department store and was looking for a new sports coat. I don't dress up much anymore, but for some reason, at the time, all my sportscoats appeared to shrink when I put them in my closet. It was the strangest thing. I would hang up my clothes in the closet, and the next time I went to put them on, they wouldn't fit! Anyway, I digress.

As I looked over the different styles, I was asked to try one on for size. I was disappointed to see that I no longer wore a 40 regular like I did when I was a pencilnecked geek at 20 years old. But this is not the salient

point...

The young woman that was helping me had her hair pulled over the right side of her face. It was styled beautifully, but it was obvious she had tried to hide the right side of her face with her flowing hair.

Her manner was professional, and her nails were meticulously polished and manicured. She dressed in great detail. Her dark Armani suit was silk with wool, and her attention to detail was unsurpassed.

Her French cuffs had been steamed with sharp creases and were crisp with perfect edges. Her cufflinks were gold…not costume jewelry; they were gold…with small rubies inset. She wore a scarf pin with the same rubies set on the clasp of solid gold.

She wore a fashion heel of five inches, unusual for a woman working on her feet all day, but she strode with confidence and intention. Her shoes were Jimmy Choo of solid black patent leather with a mother-ofpearl toe buckle.

Her hands, tanned and lovely, wore a thumb ring with three chip diamonds. Her pinky finger sparkled with yet another small diamond ring; on her index finger, she wore a silver ring with a gold inlay bearing the seal of the United States Navy.

I may wish to further describe her to have been around 5' 6" and around a size four. Her hair was coiffed perfectly...her earrings enhanced her meticulous makeup, and her lipstick was a deep ruby, lined expertly to frame her lips.

This was a beautiful woman. If you wonder how I can remember so well how she was dressed, her appearance COMMANDED my attention. She held the room...and, with no exaggeration, when she spoke...the entire department went silent. Other salespeople were watching her wait on me.

She worked efficiently, sizing me up with her eyes, and selected the exact size I needed...removing the hanger from the sports coat and expertly sliding the coat over my arms and onto my frame.

She took two small steps and stood in front of me, looking intently at my neckline, my shoulders and my face. She held a military bearing...shoulders square, eyes not wandering, but looking resolutely at my mine...communicating either approval or dismay with a single glance.

"With Your coloring...you should be wearing black or charcoal sir." she remarked with a finality that told me she was right. She removed the jacket without asking permission and selected a black velvet sportscoat out of my price range. I was going to protest, but her demeanor caused me to delay speaking.

She asked me a question that was both insightful and surgical…

"Sir, do you dress in order to blend in, or do you wish to be a force in the room when you enter?"

Her face did not smile, her eyes never deflected from mine. She was looking for an answer. She was dead serious. I had never been spoken to this way and searched my mind for an answer.

I blinked once, then twice and said, "We all wish to be a force when we enter a room, but most of the time, we are grateful if we just blend in…"

She continued to look me in the eyes and looked disappointed.

"Sir, the jacket will fit much better if you hold your shoulders back, your chin up and…" she hesitated.

"If you want to blend in, I will go get the first coat I placed on you…" then she shook her head as if to say,

"You're making a bad decision."

I asked her, "What is it? Do I not look good in the jacket?" She smiled.

"No sir...you look as if you could command the room, but your eyes betray you. Confidence comes from within...not the clothes."

I remarked to her,

"Well, if I may say this to you, you certainly command the room the way you are dressed. You have such a presence of excellence!" she beamed.

Then she pulled back her hair from around her face revealing a large deep scar. She made the comment, "I was injured when I went to rescue a fellow sailor. My face was cut by metal submerged beneath the ship from the wreck of another vessel." I was super impressed, but she didn't waver. She continued.

"I cover this side of my face, not from shame but out of courtesy to others. Confidence is a result of knowing who we truly are...and sir, if I exude excellence with a three-inch scar on my face, then when you enter a room, you should give no excuse for others to not take you seriously." My mouth fell open!

I bought the jacket, and the tie, the cuffs and the new pants. But I couldn't match her confidence, because I wasn't sure WHO I was at that time in my life.

I have sold for years, but her comments were not a ploy, not a sales tactic...she was encouraging me that who we truly are, shines through despite our outward deficiencies.

At the time, I was about forty years old, and she handed me the claim tickets to present after the tailor had done the alterations for my pants and jacket. I was to return in one week to retrieve the garments.

As I thanked her for her professionalism, she smiled for the first time and said,

"True confidence is a function of knowing who you are, and it will result in not being afraid to display that confidence regardless of circumstances." I was discipled that day by a woman with a hero's confidence. She knew who she was, and her confidence in me made me want to excel still more. Our presence on earth should make others want to be better.